Screen-Writing TRICKS OF THE TRADE

Screen-Writing TRICKS OF THE TRADE

by
WILLIAM FROUG

SILMAN-JAMES PRESS
Los Angeles

First Edition, Revised
Fourth Printing

The Joseph Wambaugh epigraph on page xv of this
book is quoted as it appeared in *Writers on Writing*
by Jon Winokur, Running Press.

Library of Congress Cataloging-in-Publication Data

Froug, William.
Screenwriting tricks of the trade / by William Froug. — 1st ed.
p.   cm.
1. Motion picture authorship. I. Title
PN1996.F772   1992   808.2'3—dc20   92-26613

ISBN: 1-879505-13-4

Cover design by Charles Field

Printed in the United States of America

SILMAN-JAMES PRESS
distributed by Samuel French Trade
7623 Sunset Blvd., Hollywood, CA 90046

To all of my former students at the University of Southern California, the University of California, Los Angeles, Danmarks Radio, and the University of Hawaii, who surely taught me as much as I taught them. Thank you, one and all, for making this book possible.

CONTENTS

Acknowledgments

To Eric Bentley, preeminent drama scholar and theorist, whose seminal work laid the foundation for this teacher to develop his own theories many long years ago; to Gwen Feldman and Jim Fox, courageous young publishers who took me off the golf course and reminded me of the joy of writing, goes my ever-lasting gratitude; master screenwriter Walter Brown Newman, painfully shy, yet always willing to share his wisdom and his tricks with struggling fellow screenwriters; the late, loquacious screenwriter William Bowers, whose hilarious and legendary stories about life as a Hollywood screenwriter were always available to aspiring young beginners—Bill spent a lifetime as a magnificent teacher without portfolio and is sorely missed by everyone in the Hollywood writing community who ever knew him; to the late movie critic and film historian Arthur Knight, who took me under his wing at the USC School of Cinema and taught me the joy of teaching; the UCLA School of Theatre Arts, Film, and Television, which provided the academic freedom and space for this novice teacher to learn and grow; and UCLA professor Lewis Ray Hunter, who drove me to distraction until I completed this book, twenty years in the making (get off my back, pal; it's done). To my children Suzy, Nancy, Lisa, and Jonathan for their ongoing and loving support. And to Christine Michaels, toughest editor of all yet still my best friend and bedazzling wife.

Foreword
by Jeffrey Boam

One of my favorite sequences in the movie *Patton* begins with the General in bed at night reading Field Marshal Rommel's book on the tactics of tank warfare. A few scenes later, Patton is presiding over a fiery battle in which his own Armored Corps has routed and out-flanked Rommel's Panzer Division. Observing the course of battle through field glasses, Patton growls gleefully (in that growl that only George C. Scott can muster), "Rommel, you magnificent bastard, I read your book."

Now, somewhere in the hills of Bel Air or along the sands of Malibu, I imagine an enterprising movie-studio executive curled up in bed poring over *Screenwriting Tricks of the Trade.* The following day, in meeting after meeting with screenwriter after screenwriter, the executive dazzles them with his deep and profound understanding of structure, character, and dramatic tension. Afterward, the bewildered writers stagger out to their cars, baking in the hot afternoon sun. They drive home in a fog, their minds reeling from the prospect that a studio executive actually knows as much about writing as they do. Meanwhile, the clever executive leans back in his chair, swings his heels up onto his desk and chuckles to himself, "Froug, you magnificent bastard, I read your book."

Of course, this is just a fantasy. This valuable book will not fall into the hands of the enemy. I know their habits and their tendencies; they will not buy and read this book. Our secrets are safe. And yet, I wish they were not. I wish every studio executive, director, producer, and agent in town would read this book. The written word is the basis upon which all work in Hollywood is done. What the screenwriter writes effects everyone who comes into the sphere of that particular project. What a wonderful world it would be if all parties involved had a true understanding of the workings of a screenplay. Okay, so much for wishful thinking.

Bill Froug is my friend, my mentor, and my one-time collaborator. We met at UCLA in the early '70s. He was my teacher and I was his student. I had the screenwriting bug, and I had it bad. I was looking at every movie I could see, reading every screenplay I could get my hands on, reading every novel that had been sold to the studios. I was trying to "get it"; trying to figure it out. Bill wasn't my first screenwriting teacher. In fact, I think he was teaching "Advanced Screenwriting 101" or something like that. (I have no memory of the classes I took or the work that I had done to qualify me for this advanced course, by the way.) I came into Bill's class with a sense of excitement fueled by the popular rumors that Bill had won an Emmy and earned over a million dollars writing and producing television programs. (Both true.) After several sessions, I decided to "target" Bill. He doesn't even know this. I made a conscious decision to impress the hell out of him. I just knew that Bill could help me, but I needed more than the slightly impersonal, two-hour-a-week instruction of the class. What I wanted was hands-on individual attention. And I got it.

During the following summer, Bill and I collaborated on a screenplay—and I received the education I came to

UCLA to find. During the course of this collaboration, Bill hammered into my head the basic and most fundamental precepts of good dramatic writing. Our battle cry was "attitude" and "tension" and "less is more" and "show it, don't say it" and "need to know." All of which Bill elaborates upon in this book. Read these sub-chapters carefully— they are short and go by fast—but I can honestly say that I have built a career on these few simple truths.

And *truths* is the word that best characterizes what Bill has written. Not rules, but truths that have emerged and revealed themselves over Bill's long, professional career. The somewhat self-deprecating title, *Screenwriting Tricks of the Trade*, is accurate. This is not a "how-to" book about screenwriting. It is a book of wisdom and good, sound advice about the *process* of screenwriting. As I read this book, the memories of receiving the benefits of Bill's experience firsthand came rushing back to me. One of the favorite tips that Bill passed on to me is not included in the following pages. Thus illustrating the old adage—Bill has forgotten more about writing than most people will ever know. At the risk of getting ahead of ourselves, I will explain this little gem right here:

Before writing a scene, imagine how you would handle that scene if you were working during the days of the silent movies. In other words, how would you tell the "story of the scene" if the characters could not speak? This has always proved to be a valuable and liberating exercise in that it instantly frees me from the bondage of the "talking heads" syndrome, keeps me from getting lazy, and forces me to find a more interesting solution to the problem of the scene.

I recall as a kid, no matter what small item I bought, there would always be a little piece of paper inside that said, "Congratulations! You have just purchased the finest harmonica (or pen-knife or compass) that money can buy!" And I think that sentiment applies to *Screenwriting Tricks of the Trade*. With this new book and his previous two books of interviews with screenwriters, with his many years of teaching filmwriting, and his long history of dedicated service to the Writers Guild, Bill has proven himself to be the screenwriter's best friend and advocate. After all, where else except in this book will you find the movie *E.T.* referred to as "Melissa Mathison's story" without any mention of you-know-who?

Jeffrey Boam
July 24, 1992

Life is a tragedy for those who feel,
a comedy for those who think.
—Jean de La Bruyère (1645-1695)

Screenwriters are like little gypsies swimming
in an aquarium filled with sharks, killer whales,
squid, octopuses and other creatures of the deep.
And plenty of squid shit.
—Joseph Wambaugh

Preface

How and Why This Book is Different From All Other Books on Screenwriting

I have on my bookshelves no less than nineteen books on screenwriting. Some are better than others. A few aren't worth the paper they are written on and a few are hopelessly out of date. Most of them say the same things in slightly different ways. And that's okay. The fundamentals of drama *are* the fundamentals of drama. The need for conflict, for example, holds true for all dramatists, which is what screenwriters are.

Yet I view the need for conflict somewhat differently than many of my colleagues. I also view structure and character development somewhat differently. Everybody's voice is as unique as their fingerprints, and it follows that mine is also.

Most books on screenwriting mention a few films and draw catchall conclusions from them. *I urge you to see any and all movies* and to *study each one* and learn how to write screenplays in the process. I will tell you exactly what to look for in each of the film you see and what lessons you can draw from them. If you know what to look for, every viewing will become an important learning experience.

I know from my twenty years of teaching screenwriting

at two of the best film schools in the United States that what I have to say will work for you. I have scores of former screenwriting students working in Hollywood, writing major motion pictures and earning huge incomes from their work, who attest to my ability to carry the message. I do not take credit for their success, but feel that my former student Jeffrey Boam put it succinctly and correctly when he told me, "You jump-started me."

My method is simple. See movies, *as many as possible*, and take from each one the important lessons that each has to offer. In the following pages I will show you exactly how to do this.

Introduction

Before there were how-to books on screenwriting, long before there were film schools, decades before there was a "film generation," there were men and women, globally, who were writing screenplays. In Hollywood, there were "stables," as the studios called them, of screenwriters plying their craft. These men and women wrote the famous films of the Thirties and Forties: *Citizen Kane, Casablanca, The Maltese Falcon, Gone With The Wind, Double Indemnity, Meet John Doe,* great movies that are still, today, the touchstones of excellence in the screenwriter's art and craft. Yet none of these talented screenwriters ever went to a film school or read a how-to book. Many of their names are legendary: Billy Wilder, Robert Riskin, Nunnally Johnson, Ben Hecht, Charles MacArthur, John Huston, Dudley Nichols, Henry and Phoebe Ephron, Carl Foreman, Herman Mankiewicz, and on and on. How did they do it?

They studied the movies that came before them. And they took the screenwriter's art up to great heights. As my good friend and prolific screenwriter Bill Bowers once told me, "We all stand on each other's shoulders."

In this book I will ask you to do as they did—study movies and learn from them.

It's all there in a treasure trove of movies, tens of thousands of them, each with many lessons to offer. (Yes, even the rotten movies. In fact, occasionally you can learn more readily from a rotten movie than from a great movie.) *If you will apply the yardsticks I will be giving you throughout this book,* you will know exactly what to look for and how to find it. You can make every movie a learning experience. I still do. I never see a film without analyzing the story structure, the core conflict, the line of action and counter-action, the opening signal, the theme, the protagonist, the antagonist, and so on. After a lifetime of writing drama and studying and teaching filmwriting, it's now second nature to me. You will find that movie-going is more fun when you're learning as you're watching. It makes for a much richer experience.

Go forward from here and be amazed by how quickly and easily you can learn what it takes to write great screenplays.

All the craft you need is in this book, but you must supply the artistry.

Although there are tens of thousands of movies available on video tape for viewing at your leisure, the best way to view a motion picture made for theatrical release is in a movie theatre, seated in a large, dark auditorium, surrounded by strangers. You get not only the communal experience but the movies as they were intended to be seen on a larger-than-life screen. You *experience* the movies as well as see them. Seeing a movie on television is like taking a bath while wearing a wetsuit.

The sad truth is that classic movies of extraordinary dimension often lose their dimension when seen on a TV screen, no matter what its size. *Citizen Kane* is the best single example. Part of the astonishing impact of Welles' masterpiece was his use of sudden shock cuts from master scene to tight close-up, frequently accompanied by loud sound effects or a musical blast from my good friend, the late Bernard Herrmann's powerful score. The shock cut to the extreme close-up of Kane's lips as he whispers his now-famous dying word "Rosebud" is but one of many examples. Those of us in the movie theatre audience in those days were nearly blasted out of our seats, as, no doubt, Welles intended. Welles was a child of radio drama and he understood the dramatic power of sound effects better than any filmmaker either before or since his dazzling debut in Hollywood. On the tube, these powerful dramatic devices are almost totally lost. Welles was a talented amateur magician and nowhere is it more apparent than in *Citizen Kane*. He introduced trick after trick that the movie audience had never seen before and has rarely seen since. Shrinking all this magic down to a few inches on a TV tube does a great disservice to this brilliant movie.

My students who saw *Kane* on video tape did not see why it's been named the greatest movie ever made by over 122 of the world's film critics, while those few who saw it in a movie theatre experienced the dramatic impact Welles intended and saw it for the classic that it is.

Movies of vast geographical scope and scenic grandeur also lose much of their impact on a TV screen. I have in mind films like *Lawrence of Arabia* and *2001—A Space Odyssey*. The latter film is totally lost on a television screen.

However, intimate stories and movies of small scope do quite well on TV, and some even improve with the shrinkage. *Casablanca* plays well on your VCR, as does *Driving Miss Daisy, Tootsie, Ghost, Home Alone, Bugsy*, etc. The more intimate the story, the better the movie plays on a TV screen. However, I do not recommend you try to study any movie by seeing it on a network or commercial television channel. By the time the hucksters get through, the film has been chopped up like so much sausage. Incredibly, some TV stations lift whole sections out of movies in order to make room for more commercials. Seeing any movie under these circumstances is not only a waste of time but a waste of a movie.

I repeat: *Every movie you see is a potential learning experience; there are no exceptions. (Even the worst ones will teach you what not to do.)*

I have divided this book into three parts with several sub-headings so you can dip in wherever you like and take from it whatever you need. The three parts are:

Thinking About the Script

Far and away the most important and time-consuming aspect of screenwriting. Some screenwriters will think about a story for years before committing it to paper. There is no standard or required time you need to work out your story problems *before* you begin to write. No matter how much time it takes, it is never wasted time. *Do not rush yourself in hopes of a quick sale* or for any other reason. In screenwriting as well as almost everything else, the old truism still holds: Haste makes waste.

Writing the Script

This, to me, is the most joyful part of the endeavor. Now I can let my characters loose, let them help me develop the story in more depth, write the dialogue, and offer me surprises. Best of all, I have the chance to surprise myself. Again, hurrying to finish the screenplay is unwise and sometimes self-destructive. Most movies are shot on a four- or five-pages-a-day shooting schedule (although seven to ten pages shot per day is not unusual for made-for-TV movies). By an odd coincidence, most screenwriting and teleplay writing comes out at about the same comparative schedule. If you can write one really terrific scene per day, you are doing very well, indeed. Sometimes, a single scene will take several days to work out properly. Although there is no standard schedule, writing four or five good pages a day is an excellent pace if you can successfully maintain it. Remember, *the quality of the work is far more important than the quantity of the work.* Don't place yourself on self-imposed deadlines. A great screenplay delivered late is *always* preferable to a mediocre screenplay delivered on time. They will always forget and forgive the lateness of a great screenplay, but you will seriously blemish your reputation by delivering a mediocre script on time.

Selling the Script

New screenwriters place far too much emphasis on selling the script and not enough on writing the script. Although their economic motives are understandable and, probably, justifiable, those who think of the money first and the screenplay second are not likely to make it in the long run. Just ask any agent whose job it is to sell your work.

Your goal must be to write the very best screenplay you can possibly write *without trying to second-guess the marketplace.* My screenwriting students who have made it big began their careers with superb samples of their work that we call "show" scripts or "calling card" scripts. Every beginning screenwriter must have at least one, or preferably several samples of his or her best efforts. Only on rare occasion did my beginning screenwriters ever sell one of their show scripts. However, if their work was outstanding, they always got an agent, and usually the agent of their choice. Some of my former students have built great careers and high-paying writing assignments for many years off of one outstanding screenplay that they wrote while students at UCLA. It is ironic that when you free yourself from being consumed by making the "big kill," the million-dollar screenplay sale, then you have the chance to free yourself to write at your highest level.

My experience with screenwriting students who pandered to what they thought the market would buy (i.e., the lowest common denominator) is that they have rarely been heard from since.

Superagents Bill Haber and Rowland Perkins are two of the co-founders of the most powerful talent agency in Hollywood, Creative Artists Agency (C.A.A.). So their words carried both wisdom and authority when they told me in *The New Screenwriter Looks at the New Screenwriter* "Tell them if they're only writing for the money, they shouldn't bother."

Outstanding talent will, by definition, stand out and eventually be recognized in Hollywood. It may not happen quickly, but it will happen. The motion picture and television industry would totally collapse if it were not for the continuous, vital and massive infusion of new talent.

There are many valuable guidelines in this book, but not rules. To exceptionally gifted artists, rules are made to be broken as they explore new ways to present their artistry. I'm all for it. Without pioneers we'd all be stuck back in the dark ages. However, few of us are exceptionally gifted enough to ignore the experience of what has worked in the past and what continues to work today. Creative pioneers lead us into tomorrow; the rest of us struggle to survive today.

But, genius or merely talent, *you cannot be boring*, under any circumstance, in any art form. That *is* a rule.

How will you know if you are committing this deadly sin? If *you* are bored as you write, I guarantee you almost everybody else will be bored as they read it (except, possibly, your mother). If you are unsure, give your finished screenplay to trustworthy friends to read, preferably those who are movie fans. Relatives are risky because they may decide to make you feel good by disguising their true feelings. Movie-going friends are usually more apt to be straightforward. In any event, get other opinions. And don't just look for reassurance; that's no help. My personal theory is, If I doubt if my script is exciting, it probably isn't.

Showing your screenplay to friends may sometimes help you when you are in doubt, but do not discuss your story with friends or with anyone else *as you are thinking about it or as you are writing it.* This is not for fear of theft. Fearing somebody will rip you off is ridiculous paranoia. There are no movie-story thieves lurking about, waiting to steal your creation, not in Hollywood nor anywhere else. The real problem is, if you tell your story-in-progress to friends, you will dissipate the energy you will need to write it. The story will become overly familiar to you, and you will gradually lose your enthusiasm for it. I had a screenwriting buddy who at a moment's notice would expound at some length about the movie he was planning to write on the Big Band era. He must have told fragments of his story to countless studio executives, agents, almost anybody who would listen. One day I asked him why he didn't stop telling it and simply start writing it.

"Are you kidding?" he replied. "Why should I write it? I'm already getting all the laughs and all the satisfaction I need *just by telling it.*"

He had hit on a profound truth. Once you get the response you want from your story, you will lose the need to write it.

The time to show your screenplay to friends is *after* you've completed it and want response, but not before it is fully developed in screenplay form.

The purpose of this book is to help you make it to the big leagues as a screenwriter. You will probably get as far as you demand of yourself.

The secret of success as a screenwriter is simple: Keep the seat of your pants to the seat of your chair. There is no substitute for hard work. Every student of mine who has made it into the big time has done so by writing screenplay after screenplay, honing his or her art and craft, getting better and better with each new script. It seems to me, on average, my students wrote at least a half-dozen feature length (120 pages) screenplays before they began to get writing assignments.

Remember that in Hollywood, as well as everywhere else on this planet, there is always room for the next generation.

During my years of teaching graduate and under-graduate level film and television writing, I worked closely with scores of beginning screenwriters, usually on a line-by-line, page-by-page basis. I was constantly amazed by how filmically sophisticated and knowledgeable they were. They often produced work of a higher order than I had seen from professional freelancers when I produced ten network television series.

Some of them, since graduating, have gone on to outstanding careers as screenwriters. About fifty of them are now working as professional writers in Hollywood and are members of the Writers Guild of America, west.

Their success has given me more pleasure than any award or honor I received during my forty-year writer-producer career in Hollywood. And a few of them I consider my close friends. Most of those fifty are working in television and have written for some of the top network television series ("LA Law," "Northern Exposure," "thirtysomething," "Cheers," "The Cosby Show," "Major Dad," "Newhart," "Anything But Love," "Coach," etc.). Here are some of my "kids" who have made the big leap into feature screenwriting, and most of them also have outstanding television credits (some of the following credits are shared).

> Jeffrey Boam — *Indiana Jones and the Last Crusade, Lethal Weapon 2, Lethal Weapon 3, The Dead Zone, Funny Farm, Innerspace, The Lost Boys, Straight Time.*
>
> Daniel Pyne — *Pacific Heights, The Hard Way, Doc Hollywood, White Sands.*
>
> Desmond Nakano — *Last Exit to Brooklyn, Boulevard Nights.*
>
> Tom Musca — *Stand and Deliver, Little Nikita.*
>
> J. Randall Johnson — *The Doors, Dudes.*
>
> Kathleen Knutsen Rowell — *The Outsiders.*
>
> Eric Roth — *Memories of Me, Suspect, The Concord—Airport '79, The Nickle Ride.*
>
> Alex Cox — *Repo Man, Sid and Nancy.*
>
> Robert R. Pool — *The Big Town.*
>
> Walter Halsey Davis — *Seven Hours to Judgement.*
>
> Gregory Widen — *Highlander, Backdraft.*
>
> Dan O'Bannon — *Alien, Blue Thunder, Return of the Living Dead, Lifeforce, Total Recall.*

Most of these screenwriters wrote many screenplays before finally selling one. Nobody ever said success comes easily. Just ask these writers.

It should be noted that, with the advent of cable, made-for-television movies, today's writers feel free to cross over from writing movies to writing TV and back again as the market dictates. Sometimes the only difference between a made-for-TV movie and a theatrical-release movie is the star casting, which always dictates big-screen budgets (star salaries are far too rich for television). A recent example is *Fried Green Tomatoes*. Before the producer had Jessica Tandy and Kathy Bates signed up, he assumed the screenplay would be a TV movie. These days, big screen, little screen, it's only a matter of budget. It's no coincidence that most of the Hollywood studios currently are headed by former network television executives.

Two other factors allow screenwriters to work the TV market without a loss of stature. In television, both the networks and the cable production companies recognize that the screenplay (ergo the writer) is the key element in their production plans, and, in the current network series, market prices per script have risen to a high enough level to make even series TV of interest to all but the most diehard screenwriters. The market is bigger and more wide open than it has ever been before. The door is closed to no one, and eager buyers await outstanding screenplays, bidding into the millions to get them.

All of the writers I've listed above have one thing in common besides their undeniable talent. They were all *absolutely* determined to become screenwriters. And, as you will learn later in this book, you just can't beat a nothing-will-stand-in-my-way protagonist. These writers' single-minded determination is more responsible for their success than anything they learned in my classroom. Determination can be an acquired attitude, available to every writer. Once you adopt the three P's—passion, patience, and persistence—you are well on your way to achieving your goal.

W. F.
Ponte Vedra Beach, FL
May 26, 1992

Thinking About the Script

O f this book's three sections, the first, Thinking About the Script, is far and away the most important. Many screenwriters think about their screenplays for months and sometimes even years before sitting down to write. This is the period of time when you make notes, think about your story, jot down possible character names, bits of dialogue, think about your theme, and, most of all, develop a strong line of action and counter-action. It is vital that you work out as many of the story problems that you can *before* you begin to write. Otherwise, you might very well fall into the writer's worst trap, writing in circles, going over and over the same material, each time with slightly different tacks leading nowhere except to endless rewriting. *Writers who go back and rewrite during the actual period of putting the screenplay on paper are doomed to never finish.* The best way to avoid this crippling error is to thoroughly think out your screenplay before sitting down to write it. No matter how much time that may take, it is time valuably spent.

Here's an important tip: if you feel a need to go back and rewrite sections or scenes of your screenplay-in-progress, make notes in the margin about the revisions you have in mind. But keep writing forward. *Do not pause to make changes.* Rewrite your screenplay *after* you have completed it. By then, you will undoubtedly have revised your thoughts about the revisions!

As the immortal pitcher Satchel Paige once said, "Don't look back, something might be gaining on you."

Very young screenwriters sometimes like to brag that they wrote their screenplay, start to finish, in ten days.

More often than not, the finished work resembles a screenplay written in ten days and little else.

Some of you may leap forward to Writing the Script in your eagerness to get started writing. I urge you not to. Writing the Script is the nuts and bolts of screenplay writing, the craft, the mechanical aspects of the job. It may, nonetheless, offer some helpful as well as disconcerting surprises. Writing a screenplay *is* fun, if you have confidence built on your preparation.

It is very helpful to know your theme before you begin to write, though it is not absolutely necessary, but you had better know it before you finish the screenplay.

How to develop a strong line of action, a strong protagonist and equally strong opposing forces, a theme, a story, etc., awaits you.

Story

A dramatic story is any series of events having *vivid, emotional, conflicting, striking* interest or results. Commit this definition to memory, then pin it up over your desk in large letters so you can view it as you develop your story. It is your litmus test. If your story meets this definition, you are well on your way toward a good screenplay. But I must add something more to the mix: It doesn't matter one bit how often your story has been told before; *you must retell it better, with a fresh and different approach.* If you can do that, your story will seem like the newest idea ever presented. Remember the eternal paradox: there is nothing new under the sun and everything is new under the sun.

Think of your story as you would a popular song. There are only a handful of notes available, yet every new hit song is unlike the ones that came before. Thousands upon thousands of popular songs are recorded, and all are variations on the same notes (and often almost the same lyrics), but each one is different enough to avoid a lawsuit. When you tell an old story in a new way, it becomes a new story.

Story Sources

Sometimes writers, novices and professionals alike, fret that they can't find a good enough story to write. I think that is from a lack of looking hard enough. We are all swimming in a sea of stories, more than we could use up in a lifetime. Here are a few great story sources that are right in front of our noses and, therefore, frequently forgotten.

(1) *Nothing is better than the feature sections of any day's metropolitan newspaper.* Great movie stories abound. Read them aloud to get the full flavor of the drama they contain. Check each one that attracts you against your dramatic litmus test. Does it have the necessary elements for a strong dramatic story? Are the vital elements ("vivid," "emotional," "conflicting," "striking") inherent in the story?

Do not worry about your legal rights to a newspaper story. By the time you turn it into a movie, it will, of necessity, have become something else, with new names, new places, and new incidents that now become the stuff of drama.

(2) *The public library is a wonderful and unlimited source for great movie stories.* One day while researching a "Gunsmoke" TV script I was assigned to write, I came across an amazing little book. It was by a Chicago reporter who had arrived on the scene of the Dalton Brothers last raid in Coffeyville, Kansas, just before the end of the 19th century. He interviewed several eyewitnesses and survivors of this audacious and foolhardy attempted double bank robbery. (The Daltons were the last of the Western outlaw gangs. All but one of them were killed in this suicidal raid. It marked the end of the Old West and the end of a chapter in American history.) I made copious notes and hurried home to work on a movie story (called a "treatment"). I sold it to United

Artists surprisingly quickly. This was simply the fallout of an afternoon in the Beverly Hills Public Library. Public libraries have so much rich material that any writer serious about his or her work can spend all the time he or she has available there.

Since the dawn of motion pictures, historical characters have been the source of countless movies. We are fascinated by the outstanding men and women of the past who have helped shape our lives today. There is no better place to find these characters in abundance than in your local library. Sometimes I feel they are almost calling out to writers, asking to be turned into movies. Spend considerable time in your local library and enjoy the feast of movie sources.

One important note of caution: Although much of the material you find in a library is in the public domain (which means the copyright has run out and it is available to any and everyone), *do not under any circumstances attempt to start your screenwriting career by adapting the work of others,* particularly novels and short stories. Professional readers will immediately see that neither the characters nor the story are yours. No matter how splendid your adaptation is, it will never be exclusively *your* original work. For this reason, I always refuse to allow my students to begin their screenwriting careers with either adaptations or in a collaboration with another writer or writers.

(3) *Building a story through a character.* Character *is* story and story is character; they are each by-products of the other. That is one reason why I highly recommend that new screenwriters begin their story search with an exceptionally strong character as subject matter. (Personally, I have found character to be the single best story-source for drama.)

Consider the great films that have come from great

characters: *Citizen Kane*, the king of them all. *Patton*, the story of the half-mad, half-brilliant World War II tank general, George Patton, who, in helping win the war in Europe, managed to almost totally destroy his career and discredit himself. *Patton* is must-see movie for all aspiring screenwriters; it shows us such a multi-faceted and complex character that it creates an archetype (we will get into type, stereotype, and archetype later). Who can top the story of arguably the greatest composer who ever lived, (*Amadeus*) Mozart? This is a brilliant play and terrific screenplay by Peter Shaffer. (The film also shows director Milos Forman at the top of his illustrious talent.) *Bonnie & Clyde* is an outstanding movie and screenplay that tells the tale of two minor outlaws of the Thirties. It is a valuable lesson for screenwriters in how to use dramatic irony to illuminate the times, place, and characters. Scores of good movies have been based on gangsters and outlaws of the Thirties, but there is a risk when you build a screenplay on a famous or infamous character.

Here is an illustration of what I mean: One summer, Jeffrey Boam came to me with exciting research material on the short life of the notorious bank robber, John Dillinger. It was a new look at a well-worn character; several movies had already been filmed about him. Nonetheless, Jeff's material was so fascinating that I agreed to collaborate on a screenplay with him, which we called *Johnny* (the name Dillinger was known by). The very day we finished the screenplay, we read on the front page of *The Hollywood Reporter* that writer-director John Milius had announced he was starting production on *Dillinger*, a film based on his screenplay about you-know-who. We were dumbfounded. But those are the breaks. *Ideas are in the air and available to anyone* who seizes them. Nobody owns the rights to current or past history. We were about six months too late. (Does it surprise you neither

Jeff nor I like Milius's version?) Nonetheless, our screenplay got raves from everyone who read it and NBC optioned it for a TV movie (it was, for the time being, dead as a feature). However, the screenplay eventually reverted to us, where it languishes sadly in our files.

One of the hidden hazards for writers in mainstream Hollywood is that they will frequently find that other writers are working on ideas similar or even identical to their own ideas. This is not plagiarism. Not surprisingly, several writers may be working on the same idea at the same time. But this is a minor risk in the scheme of things.

Plagiarism is not a frequent problem in Hollywood. And it is almost impossible to prove since you will have to prove the *other writer* had access to your material. (Unless your work has been published or widely circulated in Hollywood, you probably have no case.)

If you feel it necessary to take precautions against plagiarism, the best precaution available is to register your screenplay with the Writers Guild of America, west. It costs non-members $20. Your material will be stored and registered for five years.

No matter the risk, the lives of famous or infamous people are the stuff of great screenplays. If you've got such a project in mind, my advice is to go for it. If you don't, you'll always regret it. (It's quite possible that Jeff and I will sell *Johnny* somewhere down the line.) A completed screenplay is, as it's called in Hollywood, a property. Like a piece of real estate, there's always the chance a buyer will come along who finds it to be just what he or she is looking for. Hang on to those completed screenplays.

One day, they may be better than gold.

Let's get back to story sources.

(4) *Autobiography as story source.* Digging up incidents from your own life is a chancy business. Autobiographical material works *when you have enough distance from it to see the meaning of the experience.*

I rarely recommend young writers try to start their careers with autobiographical material. My UCLA graduate student, Gregory Widen, is a rare exception. In our seminar together, he worked on a screenplay loosely based on his experiences during his four-year career as a fireman. He called the script *Backdraft.* Sometime after graduating, he sold it to Warner's for what he told me was "a ton of money," and the movie became a big hit of the summer of '91. Greg is a serious and dedicated young writer, remarkably mature. I had no hesitation in supporting his notion to write *Backdraft.*

UCLA screenwriting student Neal Jimenez wrote several feature films before he turned to the semi-autobiographical story of his experiences in the paraplegic rehab ward for his super film *The Waterdance,* which he also co-directed. Neal's film won the Audience Award at the Sundance Film Institute and, no doubt, more awards will follow.

It is most important that young screenwriters have the courage of their conviction about the material they want to write. I never forbade a student from writing a story he or she felt strongly about.

You alone must decide what you are going to write. People (teachers, agents, etc.) who tell new screenwriters what will sell are often wrong. Nobody knows what the market will buy and nobody knows what the audience will pay to see.

Master screenwriter William Goldman said it succinctly in his book *Adventures in the Screen Trade*. When trying to figure out what the audience will pay to see, "Nobody Knows Anything," says Goldman. His book is a must-read for every aspiring screenwriter.

(5) ***The best tool of all is still a writer's notebook.*** A pocket-sized pad and pen (or tape recorder) can help you save observations that hold surprising riches. One excellent spark for stories is *overheard conversations*. I offer you two examples.

Erich Segal, author of both the best-selling novel and the hit motion-picture *Love Story*, told my USC class that he got the idea for his story when he overheard some students talking about the tragic death of another student's young wife. The idea of death occurring to one so young sparked him into writing a screenplay about it. When his agent showed the script in Hollywood, however, there were no takers. The agent suggested Erich write the same story as a novel. Erich did and the book made the top of the best-seller lists nationwide for some months. Again, his agent showed the screenplay to producers and studios, and this time they were eager buyers who paid big bucks for it. The lesson here is that Hollywood always likes to buy previously validated material. The studios and producers feel it reduces their risk.

Another example of the value of overheard conversation happened to my friend, Richard Goldstone. Dick overheard a young woman in a bar telling her friends that she had made a big-money deal to sleep with the husband of an infertile couple and give them the baby if she got pregnant. The idea of surrogate motherhood was startlingly new in the Sixties. Dick took the idea to a screenwriter, got studio backing, and produced a movie called *The Babymaker.*

(6) ***Recycling.*** There are countless story sources, yet the most popular game in Hollywood is recycling (but not for the environment). What studio executives, producers, agents, and all manner of power brokers like to recycle most is stories. If you are to work in Hollywood, you need to have a wide range of knowledge about movies. Hardly a meeting goes on without beginning with or diverting into discussions of what qualities previous movies had that made them winners and, as is more often the case, what qualities they lacked that made them losers. This is then followed by suggestions that you incorporate winning qualities from previous movies into your screenplay. (When you find yourself in such a meeting, keep your sense of humor. Intended or not, sometimes the suggestions are hilariously funny.) If you hope to participate in these professional story conferences, you'd damn well better be film literate.

The stakes are so high in the American film industry (yes, it is an industry) that hardly anyone can blame the investors for wanting to protect their investment as best they can. As of this writing, it costs almost *thirty million dollars* to produce an average-budget Hollywood movie. And that does not include prints and advertising! Some Hollywood movies cost up to sixty or even eighty million dollars to film. Star salaries, sometimes higher than eight or ten million dollars plus incredibly expensive perks, are one of the ridiculous aspects of Hollywood movie-making.

This is why recycling old material is so attractive to the studios. If they can find a formula that might guarantee success, who can blame them? Of course, the truth is, there is no formula, not for industry moguls or for screenwriters.

Write your own vision, follow your own bliss, write the best screenplay you can possibly write. Forget the market, forget pandering to your idea of what is the lowest common denominator. My students who made it to the big time did so with material *they* believed in.

It's the only way to go.

Your own imagination is still the best story source of all. Search for ideas and subject matter that is fresh, that you *haven't seen on television*. This is not an impossible task. Successful writers continually come up with concepts and stories that rocket them into big careers. Challenge yourself.

As you noodle around with random ideas and scenes, find the glue that will hold them together early on. Random scenes will not make a saleable screenplay.

The Glue

Your series of events (which we call scenes) must be held together by something that connects them, one to the other, or you have no viable story.

The something that will hold these "series of events" together like glue and turns them into a workable story is what the preeminent Greek scholar and philosopher, Aristotle, called "the imitation of an action" and what screenwriters call the "line" or the "spine." (Studio executives often call this a "through line.")

I am going to call it something closer to Aristotle's term because I want to emphasize the energy you are looking for—the power of a great, well-told dramatic story. To make your story really work, you are looking for a *single line of action.*

Action and Counter-Action

O kay, you have the subject matter and are beginning to work out the possibilities of a story. No doubt some characters are beginning to come into focus. (We will explore characters in a later chapter.) What is it that is going to make these random elements in your head into a cohesive whole that will allow you to begin to write your screenplay? It is the *action line*.

Let me give you some specific examples that will show you exactly what I mean.

As Orson Welles and Herman Mankiewicz were talking about Herman and his wife Sara's weekends at William Randolph Hearst's palatial, northern-California estate, San Simeon, they no doubt visualized Hearst, the most powerful journalist and publisher in the world, as a great character for a movie. But how could they get an audience to sit still for random scenes from the life of their surrogate Hearst, Charles Foster Kane? They had to come up with a device to hold those scenes together and, not just incidentally, hold an audience's attention. Kane's dying word, "Rosebud," was just such a device. Two reporters from "The March of Times" (never named in the film), which was the Thirties equivalent of "Sixty Minutes" in the form of a weekly theatrical newsreel and a radio series, are assigned to find the meaning of "Rosebud" and, perhaps, the meaning of Kane's tumultuous life. In the second scene of the movie, immediately following Kane's death, a detective story is set in motion. The search for the meaning of "Rosebud" is the glue that holds this Oscar-winning screenplay together.

Okay, we've got the glue and it's workable as an action line. But it is worthless unless you create *a line or lines of counter-action.* This is the *opposing force* and it is the source of the essential *dramatic tension,* without which you have no workable story or screenplay. The opposing force or forces are the roots of drama and conflict. Without conflict, you might as well pack it in—you are in the wrong field of endeavor. Without conflict, your reader will fall asleep and you will never have to think about having an audience. The ballgame is over.

What is the opposing force in *Citizen Kane?*

Ignorance. To quote William Goldman in another context, "Nobody knows anything." No matter how deeply the reporters probe, how many business associates, friends, or relatives they speak to, "Rosebud" remains a total mystery to them. The reporters never solve the riddle. But, in a stroke of genius, the co-screenwriters have the cameras slowly pull back on the dismantling of Kane's artifacts at the end of the movie, and the audience sees that Rosebud is Kane's childhood sled, probably the last thing he remembers of his brief but happy childhood with his parents. Today, everybody in the world seems to know the meaning of "Rosebud." But keep in mind as you view it again (and, I hope, still again) that nobody in 1941 had any idea of what "Rosebud" stood for.

What kept driving this movie forward and held our attention, at root, was not only the great character of Charles Foster Kane but the reporters' determination to solve the mystery of that character. *Citizen Kane* is basically an old-fashioned detective story told in an exciting and dynamic new way. (It was so new in 1941 that audiences stayed away in droves; they could not keep up with it. They were confused by its unpredictable, non-sequential structure that was decades ahead of its time.) Fifty-plus years later, those very same dynamic elements remain fresh and exciting. The opposing force that keeps us glued to this mystery is that, as with all good mysteries, we have a need to know the answer to the riddle. What keeps us from knowing *are the opposing forces.*

William Goldman took the story of two lesser-known Western outlaws, Butch Cassidy and the Sundance Kid, and created a highly entertaining and astonishingly successful movie. A lot of writers knew about Butch and Sundance, but only Goldman knew what to do to make them into the highest purchase-price original screenplay ($400,000) of its time (1969). He knew the story of two outlaws heading for Bolivia to rob banks was not, in and of itself, a workable screenplay. He had a great line of action (going to Bolivia), but there's no dramatic tension in that endeavor. No matter how charming Butch and Sundance were (and God knows Goldman made them charming), he needed something else, a strong counter-action. So he did what any world-class screenwriter would do, he invented The Superposse led by the greatest tracker in the history of the West (a perfect opposing force for this story). Now he had both the action line and the counter-action line, and they were, as they should be, *on a collision course.*

Let's consider *Ferris Bueller's Day Off*—one of the funniest comedies of the past decade—a must-see for new screenwriters. Nothing better illustrates the essential values of a line of action and an opposing force. Ferris is determined to play hookey from school for the day and drag along two of his reluctant schoolmates (their *oppo-*

sition provides many of the laughs). Ferris has planned all this with the cunning of a general going into a major battle. As he implements his nefarious plan, the audience learns that the school principal is onto Ferris and is determined to nail him. For every move Ferris makes, the principal (in a hilarious performance by Jeffrey Jones) makes a counter-move.

Self-destruction

A far more interesting and complex type of interaction between a line of action and opposing forces is self-destruction. Here are some examples of it in action.

Bugsy — A gangster is determined to make himself an important force in Hollywood, even to the extent of trying to become a movie star. That's the line of action. Inventing Las Vegas is part of that scheme. The line of counter-action is that he's crazy. He finally causes his own destruction.

Stories about self-destruction are often the stuff of √√ great movies because the lines of action and the opposing force are *built into the characters.*

Clean and Sober, Drugstore Cowboy, The Days of Wine and Roses, Postcards from the Edge, The Lost Weekend are all examples of characters who try to survive (the line of action) against their addiction, their need to self-destruct (the opposing force). Sometimes the disease wins; sometimes the healthy aspect of the character wins. It is the √√ classic and enduring battle between good (God) and evil (the devil). It is a battle everybody can relate to, which is why it works so well in drama.

Watch how quickly the line of action begins in every movie you see and how soon the opposing force is established. This is a very important way to view movies.

Here are some examples of movies with strong lines of action and counter-action.

The Black Robe — A Canadian priest goes into the wilderness to bring Catholicism to the native Indians (line of action). They fight against him and his religion (opposing force).

A line of action is no good unless you also have at least an equally strong opposing force.

JFK — New Orleans D.A. Jim Garrison becomes obsessed with solving the riddle of President John F. Kennedy's assassination (line of action). He gathers a wealth of bits and pieces of information, but they will not add up to enough to make a case and he constantly hits a wall of indifference, disbelief, and hostility (opposing forces).

Thelma and Louise is the often-told tale of two outlaws on the run, except that, in this telling, they are both women. They begin their odyssey as a lark, as a chance to get a holiday from their male-dominated lives. The lark becomes a killing and we are off on a chase-the-outlaws movie. The line of action is two women seeking escape from their respective oppressive males, and the opposing forces are the cops trying to catch them.

Casablanca — A nightclub owner whose club has become the gathering place for opposing forces during World War II is determined to remain neutral. That is Rick's *line of action.* Everybody else he comes in contact with, including his former girlfriend, are *determined to force him to take sides.* That is the line of action and the opposing forces that hold this movie together.

Patton — Francis Coppola's and Edmund North's Academy Award-winning screenplay is not primarily about how General George Patton helped win the war against the Germans. The line of action is Patton's determination to impose his will and his views on everyone around him, including his superiors. The line of counter-action is that Patton's views are wildly out of sync with those of his superiors. He becomes a liability instead of an asset to the Allies and thereby defeats himself.

The Godfather — Another character who is determined to enforce his will on everyone around him. That is the line of action. The opposing forces are the other people, Mafia families, who will not bend their will to his.

Almost all Private Eye, Cop, or Western movies work on the strength of their single line of action and the strength of their opposing force. You can make book on it.

The following are recent examples of major Hollywood movies that failed to achieve their potential because they had no single line of action or counter-action:

Prince of Tides — Originally a story of a man going to New York in an effort to help his sister who is recovering from a suicide attempt. Single line of action, right? In the movie version, this man (Nick Nolte) goes to New York, falls in love with his sister's psychiatrist, gets into a relationship with her (Barbra Streisand), and the line of action becomes, Will he or won't he return to his wife? The film loses much of its audience and positive critical response when the line of action is bent in an entirely different direction. The sub-plot takes over the major plot, which is not a good idea.

Grand Canyon — Lawrence Kasdan, who wrote the superb *Body Heat* and the fascinating *Big Chill,* misses with *Grand Canyon* because it has no single line of action or counter-action, only a lot of splendid scenes, each with their own line of action. The theme of the film remains murky. Kasdan's *The Big Chill,* which is also a study of a group of people, was held together by the Aristotelian concept of the three unities of time, place, and theme. These three unities *became* the line of action: How do we cope with the cold reality of death and life after college?

Of growing up? All of the characters were facing the same *line of action.* The line of counter-action is their mutual confusion and uncertainty, their inability to cope.

Two thousand years from the grave, Aristotle still speaks to us and speaks the truth. Read Aristotle's *Poetics* and you will find gems as valuable to the modern screenwriter as they were to the ancient Greek dramatists.

What applies to musicians, artists, ballet dancers, and practitioners of all arts applies to screenwriters: In order to create viable art that will hold someone's attention, you must have *dramatic tension.* Which, in screen-writing, is created by a line of action and opposing forces. Tension = Attention.

It is obvious that screenplays have many more elements than a single line of action and counter-actions. What is important for the aspiring screenwriter to know is that great screenplays *have* a single line of action and equally powerful opposing forces.

If you have a strong line of action and strong opposing forces, they can support any number of scenes, sub-themes, sub-plots, whatever you need. Sub-plots are usually dictated by the strength of your characters. They are important to filling out your main story line, *if* they do not take over and turn your line of action in a new direction.

American movies dominate the world marketplace and are enormously popular almost everywhere on the planet. I believe it is our dynamic storytelling style that captures the world-wide public. Our movies are energized by strong lines of action and counter-action. It's that simple. Compare our movies to those from other countries and you will see our "secret for success" is no secret. It's right up there on the screen.

As you have been working out your story, you have,

no doubt, begun to focus on *your approach* to the material. In what style do you want to tell this story? Do you see it as a comedy, a melodrama, a farce, or a lower-key (sometimes called "natural") drama? The decision you make determines the *kind* of movie you will write, the *genre*.

With minor adjustments, every story can be told in any genre you choose.

What Is It?

As you are working on your story, decide which of the fundamental genres suits this particular story. Here are six basic drama genres.

(1) **Drama**, itself, we have already defined as "any series of events having vivid, emotional, conflicting, striking interest or results" (which I hope you have chiseled in stone over your desk). There are some other definitions of drama worth mentioning. My favorite is, "Drama is life with all the dull stuff taken out."

The great German philosopher Goethe said, "Art is art because it is not life," and good drama is most certainly a high art.

The drama scholar, playwright, and critic Eric Bentley accurately observed that "drama is the art of exaggeration." To which I would add: It is also the art of compression.

Facts are the stuff of documentarians and historians, and both are all too often boring. The truth behind the facts is what the dramatist seeks. In a sense, we writers are, at our best, gifted liars. We put order and structure around our stories about life when, in fact, life most often has no structure and is frequently chaotic. Audiences love good drama because *it imposes order* on the chaos of life.

Search for the drama in your story. Find the big scenes, the big moments. Some screenwriters feel that if they have ten or fifteen "high" (dynamic, highly emotional) scenes in a screenplay, they have a movie. With some reservations, I think they are right. I'd rather see you chew the scenery in your writing than be a shrinking violet hoping some character will come along and rescue you. I spent several years directing actors in radio drama. I learned from experience that you could always tone down an actor's tendency to overact. It was never a problem. But there was little you could do for the actor whose first reading badly underplayed the material. Getting them up to a performance was like pulling teeth. So it is with writers. Those who tip-toe softly through their material rarely succeed. Those who come on strong, bold, going for the big scenes, the big moments, are the ones most likely to make it. In building your story, push it to the limits, push your characters to their limits, make the big scenes bigger. It's always easier to cut back than to add on.

(2) *Melodrama* is exaggerated drama. It emphasizes action over character and is the most common genre shown on television. Melodrama is laced with gunfights, fistfights, car chases, murders, and violence. A lot of critics put anything in this genre down as inferior work. I don't agree. Nothing is more violent than nature itself. Our solar system was born of violence, as was Earth. Violence is an integral part of human existence. The ancient Greeks gave their audiences plays dripping with blood and violence. Watch the evening news on television or read any day's newspaper to recognize that we live in a violent world.

My former UCLA student Judith Kanner pointed out in an interesting article in the *Los Angeles Times* that we have come a long way from the ancient Romans who brought out huge crowds with bloody exhibitions of live human slaughter and dismemberment by the gladiators. Our modern equivalent, pro football, gratefully, is tepid by comparison.

Movie audiences clearly love melodrama or there would be no Arnold Schwartzenegger, Sylvester Stallone, and all our other super-jock heroes. The cautionary note here is that there is so much melodrama floating around these days that the burden on the screenwriter to be original is even greater. Melodrama is, in some ways, the easiest genre to write, but it is also the most difficult to do in a fresh, compelling way.

(3) **Comedy** is a *form of drama* and has the same requirements as drama. Comedy must have a strong storyline with strong conflict—striking, vivid, emotional, etc. The only difference between comedy and drama is that comedy requires that the story be told in a humorous way and have a happy ending. Any straight dramatic story can be told as a comedy.

When I produced half-hour sitcoms ("Bewitched," "Gilligan's Island") for network television, writers meetings would usually begin with some joke telling, clowning around, until the time came to say, "Come on, guys, let's get serious here. We're working on a comedy series." We then began the real story conference by asking the writer or writers what the storyline was. And the line had to have a strong conflict in it. Charlie Chaplin took this a step further—he believed cruelty is an integral part of comedy. He often based his feature-length comedies on *tragic situations* (*City Lights, The Gold Rush, The Great Dictator, Monsieur Verdoux,* etc.)

The surpassing genius in the history of motion pictures, Chaplin defined genre distinctions with telling simplicity. He once gave this example to make his point: A man falls down a flight of stairs, breaks his neck, and dies. That's a tragedy. The same man falls down a flight of stairs and is only bruised, hops up, dusts himself off, adjusts the flower in his lapel, walks off jauntily down the street. That's a comedy.

Chaplin said that he began thinking about his comedies by thinking about tragic situations. Example: While thinking about the Donner party who, lost and starving to death in the High Sierra, in utmost desperation ate the bodies of their frozen comrades. "Ah," Chaplin said, "*cannibalism!* The perfect foundation for a comedy!" (See *The Gold Rush* and see how the master turned cannibalism into one of the funniest scenes ever filmed.)

Your *attitude* toward every story idea that comes to you will tell you which genre best suits a particular idea.

(4) **Farce** is exaggerated comedy. It is comedy pushed to the limits of absurdity. Classic movie farces include *Dr. Strangelove, A Funny Thing Happened on the Way to the Forum, M*A*S*H, Blazing Saddles, Support Your Local Sheriff, The Producers* (one of the funniest movies ever made).

Dr. Strangelove is a must-see movie for every beginning screenwriter. Not only is it a brilliant farce, it also shows us the unique ability of this genre for political satire. It packs a most powerful message. A screenwriting lesson embodied in this movie is how readily a strong, dramatic, storyline adapts to hilarity and outrageous humor. It is said that this movie was originally planned as a straight drama until someone at Columbia Pictures realized that they were also developing another drama with an almost identical storyline: *Fail Safe.* Terry Southern, a highly regarded novelist comedy writer, was then brought in on the *Strangelove* screenplay, and it became an enduring farce.

(5) **Tragi-comedy**. This genre is self-descriptive. It blends, or interweaves, comedy and tragedy, usually ending it tragic consequence. *Dr. Strangelove* fits this genre also because of its ending, whereas *M*A*S*H* and the other farces mentioned above, which all had happy endings, do not. Other examples of this genre are *Oh! What*

a Lovely War and *City Lights.*

(6) ***Tragedy*** is a genre rarely seen in contemporary American movies because the studios and the financiers fear that the public will not pay to see a heavy-duty downer. A tragedy is a story in which the protagonist brings about his own downfall. Shakespeare's tragedies include *King Lear, Hamlet,* and *Othello.* Eugene O'Neill's *Long Day's Journey into Night* is a great contemporary tragedy, as is Arthur Miller's *Death of a Salesman.*

Bridge on the River Kwai is a tragedy. So is *A Bridge Too Far* and *Butch Cassidy and the Sundance Kid,* although each of these films has many comedic moments. (As Chaplin proved again and again, there is comedy in tragedy.)

You can mix genres within your screenplay; it's done all the time. Drama with a touch of comedy is almost standard fare. The same for comedy with a touch of farce.

No matter what genre you choose, what's important is that you establish it on page one of your screenplay.

Next: The human species' second most popular activity—people-watching.

Character

While you're noodling around in your mind with your story ideas ("notions" as many screenwriters call them), you will no doubt be shopping for the character who will carry your story, the protagonist. You will need a character who is strong and fascinating. Wimps need not apply.

The Protagonist

The protagonist is the character who carries your story and is the focal point of your screenplay. (The Greeks called this character the hero.)

There may be several protagonists if they are all following the same line of action.

Choosing Your Protagonist

First, let's dispense with an ugly rumor: your protagonist does *not* have to be likable. You do *not* have to create a "rooting interest" in her or him. These are ugly rumors that kill off a lot of promising stories and a lot of promising writers who instinctively know better.

What you must create is a protagonist who is *fascinating, compelling, interesting, and understandable.* Off-the-beaten-path characters are almost invariably much more interesting than run-of-the-mill, solid citizens. (Hitchcock used an interesting formula in many of his movies: ordinary citizens get caught up in extraordinary situations and are forced to take extraordinary action. This formula has been overworked since Hitchcock's use of it, which may be the reason why so many of Hitchcock's movies seem dated.)

Here are some examples of strong movie characters who display the traits that I'm talking about.

Is Scarlett O'Hara likable? Hardly, but we understand "where she's coming from" and why she does what she does. That's what counts. How about Charles Foster Kane, Rick in *Casablanca*, Sam Spade in *The Maltese Falcon*, Fred C. Dobbs in *The Treasure of the Sierra Madre*? Are any of these characters "likable"? Add George Patton, Bonnie Parker and Clyde Barrow, Robert De Niro as the *Taxi Driver*, either Thelma or Louise, Sigourney Weaver in all three *Alien* movies, and on and on. How about Jack Nicholson in *Chinatown* or any Nicholson role? Nicholson has achieved superstardom playing unlikable characters, as have Bogart, Cagney, George C. Scott, and many of our most successful and gifted actors. Successful movies are most often made from dynamic characters who are utterly *fascinating* and whose behavior is often not likable, but is understandable.

A recent example of the disaster of "likability" as a yardstick for movie success came when Warner Bros. executives insisted on casting likable Tom Hanks as the unlikable protagonist, Sherman McCoy, in the film of Tom Wolfe's novel *Bonfire of the Vanities*. "Likable" was perhaps the major reason why the movie was a notable Hollywood disaster. Read Julie Salamon's superb documentation on the making (or unmaking) of a major Hollywood fiasco. There has never been a better account of how Hollywood works than Ms. Salamon's book, *The Devil's Candy*.

Insecure movie executives, agents, producers, and directors (who can blame them for wanting to guarantee success?) like to come at a screenplay with the uppermost question in their minds: "Is your lead 'likable'?" Remind them that almost all of the really great movies and the Oscar-winning movies (many of which are not great, by the way) are made from screenplays with powerful, *compelling* protagonists who, unlikable or not, nonetheless, *rivet the attention of the audience.*

Okay, you've got the makings of a character; now, how do you get him or her to take action, *to do*, to create your screenplay?

Create the "something" or someone he or she *must have or passionately wants.*

Jessica Tandy playing a prickly, unlikable, wealthy, older woman *is determined to maintain her independence* in spite of her advancing age and *will not accept* dependence on a chauffeur (Morgan Freeman). Out of this simple but dynamic line of action comes the Oscar-winning *Driving Miss Daisy.* In this movie, Miss Daisy's son (Dan Aykroyd) provides the opposing force—he *insists* on the chauffeur and will not take no for an answer.

If your must-have character's determination is to have another character of the same or opposite sex, you have a love story or a lust story depending on how you choose to write it. Love stories are never out of fashion, they merely change style. *Ghost*, Bruce Joel Rubin's Oscar-winning screenplay, was a big hit recently. It's an ordinary love story with an unordinary ghost. This ghost element gave the script what agents call "spin," something offbeat, *different*, yet still with the ordinary elements of a love story. ("Spin" is the current Hollywood catchphrase to describe what screenwriters need to create a breakthrough screenplay sale; something just a little different that will separate it from all the others.)

A great character is *always* different. No two people are identical, not even "identical" twins. If you dig deeply into your character, really explore what drives him or her, you will have a leg up on a fine screenplay.

A word of caution: beware of rewriting a character you have seen in a previous movie, *unless you have a new and fresh approach.*

It was not uncommon at UCLA to find lazy writers who leaned on late-night TV movies as their chief source of research and inspiration. My suggestion is: *don't.* If you want to rework an old story, you must reconceptualize it, make it new. This is especially true when dealing with characters from old movies. Great characters are all around us. We do not need to look to old movies as a source.

Great characters are not difficult to come by if you keep your eyes and your ears open. Look into your local political scene; there's a good chance you might find some fascinating characters in that crowd. Look for the *exceptional people* in your workplace or your neighborhood. It's a very good place to begin.

Here are some great movie protagonists. I recommend that you study them.

Lawrence of Arabia, Citizen Kane, Patton, Tootsie, Raging Bull, Bonnie & Clyde, Gorillas in the Mist (Dian Fossey).

Approaching a Character

How do you approach a character? First, it depends on the genre you chose for your story—comedy, melodrama, tragedy, tragi-comedy, etc. Having chosen a genre for your particular story, you must now decide on the "take" for this character.

The take on a character is the slant, the angle, the beat, or approach the screenwriter takes on his or her character. You can see how marvelously driven characters work by studying *The African Queen* with Bogart and Hepburn. Both characters are determined to go in opposite directions. (Neither of them are remotely likable, but both are completely understandable.) She insists they go down river and sink the German gunboat; he insists on drinking his gin and riding out the war in his little boat. He thinks the mission is nonsense; she won't take no for an answer. This is a perfect mating of two dynamic, strong-willed opposites forced, by circumstance, into cramped quarters. There is no escape from each other. They are trapped in the same boat. This is the power of the *unity of opposites*. The *African Queen's* Academy Award-nominated screenplay is by one of our greatest authors and film critics, the late James Agee. Read the screenplay. Everything you want in a great screenplay is there. This is a must-see movie for every aspiring screenwriter.

Neil Simon's *The Odd Couple*, an Oscar-nominated screenplay by the master of contemporary comedy, is another unity-of-opposites story in which two characters are confined in a given space (an apartment), each *determined* to live his own distinct lifestyle. It's a lesson in how to write a "buddy picture." Make note that the key element is this movie is the humor derived from *conflict*.

Writing for Actors

Since the dawn of drama, writers have been writing roles with specific actors in mind. We have no details of this practice among the ancient Greek dramatists, but we have records of dramatists (from Shakespeare to Shaw to Arthur Miller and Tennessee Williams) who clearly had a certain actor or actress in mind as they wrote their plays. It's a very good idea, and very helpful in the writing process, to have a vision of an important player as you write. This may also prove to be quite helpful in selling your screenplay. (This only applies when you are writing for big-name stars who can attract an audience.) When you have finished and polished your screenplay and are ready to send it off to an agent, put the names of the actors that you have in mind in your cover letter. If the agent likes your screenplay, he or she will get it to that particular actor. This could be a leg-up, not only in the writing but in the hoped-for sale.

If you have a director in mind who you think would be especially right for this particular screenplay, include his or her name in your cover letter as well.

All movie characters are made up of bits and pieces of many people the screenwriter has observed with a dash of himself or herself thrown in. Your character is then pushed to the limits by *very difficult circumstances* created by the writer. The more difficult the circumstances, the more the character is forced to reveal herself or himself in dramatic or comedic ways. Difficult circumstances create *conflict*, the lifeblood of all screenwriters.

A delightful movie that illustrates this point is *Meeting Venus*. It is the story of a Hungarian conductor brought to Paris to conduct Wagner's *Tannhauser*. Everything and everybody attempts to thwart this character's single-minded determination to conduct this performance. Out of *this single line of action* comes a very funny comedy that hides its craft under a richly textured blanket of artistry. I highly recommend it to new screenwriters. Alas, the backers seemed to abandon the film almost simultaneously with its release. No ads, no promotion. It was not released, it escaped. As a consequence, in Hollywood parlance, "It didn't open."

How To Know Your Protagonist

How much do you need to know about your protagonist before you write her or him? The answers differ depending on which screenwriters you talk to. Some writers feel they need a complete biography of their protagonist before they can begin to write. They even begin by writing a detailed history of the character's ancestors, then onward from birth to the present. Lillian Hellman, a famous playwright, felt she needed to know as much as possible about her characters in order to write them.

Most screenwriters I have known and worked closely with feel they need to know only enough so that they can see and hear their characters in their mind's eye. This is my approach, too. If I can see and hear my characters talk, *all of them*, there is nothing else I need to know. They become vivid and alive in my mind's eye. I know their behavior and attitudes, and that's all I need to know. If I need more, the characters will surely reveal themselves to me as my story demands it. I suggest you do not over-analyze your characters. I believe that the single most important thing for screenwriters to achieve is a level of intimacy with their characters that will allow the characters to talk to them. This is the greatest thrill a screenwriter can know. This is being in *total empathy and intimacy with your characters*. I have frequently written a scene and typed with both delight and amazement as the characters seemingly dictated their dialogue. Frequently, I have laughed out loud at something funny one of the characters has said, without having the slightest awareness that I am creating it.

When you have this degree of intimacy with your characters, you will write with the unique joy of creativity. When you write at this level, you are never alone—your characters are always available to you. (There are times when I wonder what is presently happening to characters

I created in scripts some years ago. They are that real to me.)

In great screenplays, the characters come to life on the page. Know your characters, all of them, *before you write your screenplay.* Try to bring even minor characters to life, give them a little something extra, a touch, a bit of business that makes them "real." Avoid the ordinary as you would the plague.

It must be noted that professional readers, at no matter what level of the hierarchy, when reading your screenplay, will *immediately know* if your characters are speaking for themselves or if you are putting words in their mouths. Well-written characters come that much to life, even on the printed page. As you are writing, you must ask yourself, Am I writing this dialogue or are my characters speaking for themselves? *This is an absolutely critical point.* If you force dialogue into your characters' mouths, they will be dull and lifeless. Count on it.

Here are some things you can ask yourself that will help you to reach the needed level of intimacy with your characters.

Type

In what ways is this character a type? A cop like other cops, a student like other students, a teacher like other teachers, etc.? Establish the character's *type.*

Caution: Writers who stop there have a dull, lifeless, one-dimensional character, one of the deadliest sins of poor screenwriting.

Types can be useful in very minor roles. Producers and directors will frequently resort to "typecasting" in minor parts. Thus, in movies, you will frequently see cops who look like the public's idea of what a cop should look like. The same is often true with bankers, students, teachers, blue-collar, and white-collar workers. Typecasting is a form of shorthand that will signal a wide range of information at a glance. Nonetheless, I urge screenwriters to put some special twist or spin on what would ordinarily be a "type character." The simplest twist can make what might be a dull scene fresh and interesting. Dan Pyne did this successfully when he was called in to rewrite *Doc Hollywood.* He gave the small-town mechanic a computer capability and sophistication well beyond our expectations and added interesting and unexpected touches to several other minor characters. It's not difficult to enhance types by finding that something extra that turns the ordinary into the special. Work for it—it will enhance your career and your reputation.

Uniqueness

The next level you need to explore in knowing your character is, in what ways is she or he like no other cop, no other student, no other teacher, etc.? In short, *in what ways is this character unique?* Find these elements, and you are heading toward building a terrific character.

Universality

Finally, and just as importantly, you must know in what ways your character is *like every other human being* on the planet. *Universal characteristics* are extremely important. These will allow us to readily *recognize* your character as "one of us." It opens the door for both your and the reader's *empathy.* Empathy comes when you *understand* the characters. Thus we can say, in some ways, *we are them and they are us. To recognize* means *to know again.* Some universal characteristics are that we all try to eat when we are hungry, sleep when we are tired, laugh when we are joyful, cry when we are hurting. Even the worst villain does these things and becomes recognizable as a fellow human being in spite of his or her unsavory nature.

This is what you must demand of yourself when you are writing characters. Anything less puts you among the also-rans.

Stereotypes

Stereotypes are exaggerated types that are very useful for the screenwriter working in the genres of farce and tragi-comedy; but they are the kiss of death in drama, melodrama, and tragedy. Stereotypes are types brought to the level of the absurd. They generally provoke laughter when they are intended for humor and disgust when they are used in serious drama. Stereotypes are especially useful for political satire. Classic examples of successfully employed stereotypes are found in *Dr. Strangelove, A Funny Thing Happened on the Way to the Forum* (stereotypes on display with hilarious results), and *The Producers.*

Archetype

Your goal with your protagonist is to *create* an *archetype*, an original pattern, the prototype. Or, in the Jungian sense, "a collectively inherited idea, pattern of thought, image." Thus, one can say about the movie character based on the real General George Patton, "Yes, I recognize him, he behaves like my idea of how generals behave." If you stopped there, you would have only a type. A strong writer digs much deeper—he or she tells you *what else* there is about the character that makes him or her absolutely unique, one-of-a-kind, while at the same time being like all other generals. This is what separates the mediocre writers from the exceptionally gifted writers. Become the latter; look so deeply into your character that your reader or audience can say, "Yes, I recognize him or her, but I have never seen him or her like this before." This is your challenge and your goal. *People are complex*; your characters should reflect this fact of life.

Consistent Characters

The term is an oxymoron. There is no such thing as a "consistent" character. Item: a mild-mannered Texas college student goes up into a campus tower with a high-powered rifle and shoots a dozen people, killing several. He is a straight-A student with an exemplary behavioral record. ("He wouldn't hurt a fly.") Item: a mild-mannered guy in San Diego (good husband, good worker, Mr. Average Citizen) goes to a McDonalds and shoots up the place, killing and wounding many people. It happens often, and the killer's friends and neighbors almost always describe him as a quiet, mild-mannered neighbor who was "never a problem."

But people get into stressful situations to the point of being overwhelmed, and then they are capable of committing all sorts of outrageous acts that nobody would have thought them capable of committing.

The job of the dramatist is to create those stressful situations that *cause people to behave "unlike themselves."*

I am particularly fond of the great Russian novelist Leo Tolstoy's description of character: "One of the most widespread superstitions is that every man has his own special, definitive qualities, energetic, apathetic, etc. Men are not like that . . . men are like rivers . . . every river narrows here, is more rapid there, here slower, there broader, now clear, now cold, now dull, now warm. It is the same with men. Every man carries in himself the germs of every human quality, and sometimes one manifests itself, sometimes another, and the man often becomes unlike himself, while still remaining the same man."

People are infinitely complicated; and whatever they do may be for an infinite number of reasons, many of them unfathomable to others and even to themselves.

Motivation

I like what screenwriter Walter Newman (uncredited for *The Great Escape* and *The Magnificent Seven*, co-screenwriter of *Cat Ballou, The Man with the Golden Arm*, and several others) had to say on the subject of knowing your character's motivation in our interview in *The Screenwriter Looks at the Screenwriter.* "There is a building burning and a mother is distraught on the sidewalk, and some passerby hears her say that her child is inside, and he rushes into the building and rescues the child, puts it down, and walks away. What was his motivation? I have no idea. I know what his *purpose* was, but nothing more. I think that motivation is conversational coinage that directors pass around, and I see no value in exploring motivations for characters."

Writing a Test Scene

Here's a trick that can help you discover if you know enough about your protagonist to write him or her. Pick out a scene from any section of your projected script that features your protagonist and *write it first*. It will give you a measure of your feel for the character. *There is no law that says you must always start writing your movie on page one.* Some screenwriters begin writing in the middle and progress in both directions over the weeks or months of the writing process. Write your particular story in the manner that is best for you. Nobody is looking over your shoulder (or most certainly should not be).

The Antagonist

In most movies, the opposing force is another person, a villain. In real life, few of us are either all black or all white; almost all of us are some shade in between, a shade of gray. Movie villains are often not like that. It would make for more interesting drama if they were, but the audiences seem to like their villains totally evil. Cheering the hero and hissing the villain has never gone out of fashion. As witness, Martin Scorsese's remake of *Cape Fear*, a pedestrian 1962 melodrama turned into a pedestrian 1991 melodrama also called *Cape Fear*. In Scorsese's remake, Robert De Niro plays a villain who is the devil incarnate. He is completely evil with no redeeming virtues. The movie racked up big box-office grosses, no doubt on the basis of this utterly black-hearted villain. Apparently, in both domestic and foreign movies, you can't get too villainy to displease an audience. Writers take note: Scorsese is often called "America's greatest director" on the strength of a body of work in which all the characters in his movies are various degrees of wicked and miserable people.

While watching villains, perhaps members of the audience are telling themselves, "Isn't he (or she) awful; I'm glad I'm not like that." Watching villainy lets people vent their rage in a harmless way. You may feel the same way as you write these black-hearted rogues. There is an element of *fun* in the process.

Thus, you need impose no limits on your creation of the opposing force if she or he is a villain *in a melodrama*. Glenn Close played a fire-breathing villain in the box-office hit *Fatal Attraction*. The actions of both her character and that of Robert De Niro's in *Cape Fear*, no matter how ferocious and improbable, are nonetheless totally understandable to the audience. This element of understandability is necessary for villains of all stripe and all genres. The entire output of James Bond movies attests to how outrageous the villains in melodramas can be, and must be.

(Of course, there's a whole catalog of opposing forces other than fellow human beings.)

The Straw Man

It is important that whoever or whatever your villain is in a melodrama, he, she, or it must be the *most dangerous* villain imaginable. The villain or opposing force must seem *much stronger* than your protagonist. All of the *Superman* movies vividly demonstrate how hard it was for the writers to create an opposing force to be a serious threat to Superman. The danger of a weak villain cannot be overstated. This little fable will illustrate my point.

Back in the Age of Chivalry, when knighthood was in flower, there was a powerful knight who defeated every opponent he met in the jousts. He boasted that he would take on any challenger in the land. A plot was hatched by the various knights' pages. For the coming match, the pages took a suit of armor and stuffed it with straw, then tied it to a mighty steed. The king signalled the start of the contest, the great superknight saw his opponent enter the field, helmet down, galloping toward him. With a courtly bow, he whirled and rode to meet the challenger. There was a clash and clatter of armor, the challenger hit the ground, and the superknight pranced around, waving his lance triumphantly. But, instead of the expected applause, there were jeers and boos. Dumbfounded, the superknight looked back toward the defeated "challenger" and saw only scattered armor and straw. The superknight retreated from the field humiliated. He had defeated a straw man.

Unless the threat is deadly serious, it's a joke and your protagonist will be ridiculed.

Think of Rocky going into the ring for a championship fight. He throws one punch and his opponent drops down to the canvas, out cold. It's a big laugh.

A straw man can sabotage your screenplay. The dramatic tension of your story hinges not so much on the power of your protagonist as it does on the power of your antagonist, your *villain*. Weak villains will undercut your story and leave it limp and lifeless. As the success of *Cape Fear* attests, thoroughly evil, wicked, and clever-beyond-all-measure villains are still what holds an audience enthralled. This is absolutely true in the genre of melodrama. However, in drama there is plenty of room for subtlety.

Opposing Forces

Here are some opposing forces, other than a single antagonist, that create terrific dramatic tension and conflict in a screenplay.

A person against themselves: Anna Hamilton Phelan's excellent, Oscar-nominated screenplay for *Gorillas in the Mist* about the great ape researcher Dian Fossey. Ms. Fossey was murdered in her sleep, but she was responsible for her own death because her fanatic devotion to the great apes drove her to make enemies of everybody with whom she came in contact.

A person or people against nature: All disaster movies, trek movies (defined as a person or people on an arduous journey together) involve characters who struggle against the forces of nature as well as each other.

A person or people against the system: Paddy Chayefsky, arguably the greatest screenwriter in the history of the movies, was peerless in his screenplays portraying characters frustrated by the corporations and institutions to which they were emotionally committed: *The Hospital*, a brilliant, insightful, and ruthless look at the current state of metropolitan hospitals; and *Network*, Chayefsky's insightful and devastatingly accurate take on the way our television networks operate, are both prime examples.

*M*A*S*H* is, essentially, a ribald look at the U.S. Army in wartime Korea. The antagonist is not the North Korean

Army, it is the madness of the institution of war.

Bridge on the River Kwai is a classic movie whose theme is also the utter insanity of war and how the madness affects and infects the characters. A great movie.

Buddy Movies

If two protagonists follow the same line of action, this is, in Hollywood parlance, a "buddy" picture. Examples are: *Thelma and Louise, Butch Cassidy and the Sundance Kid, The Odd Couple, Midnight Cowboy, Driving Miss Daisy*, and *Lethal Weapon* and its sequels. Hollywood has a long-standing and abiding love affair with buddy pictures and so does the audience.

Who is the protagonist in these "buddy pictures"? Susan Sarandon or Geena Davis? Paul Newman or Robert Redford? Jack Lemmon or Walter Matthau? Mel Gibson or Danny Glover? Jessica Tandy or Morgan Freeman? In all of these movies, *both characters* are the protagonists, yet they are quite *different* from one another. They always have opposing points of view, which is what provides both the conflict and the humor.

Ron Bass's Academy Award-winning screenplay for *Rain Man* perfectly demonstrates the rich conflict and humor you can gain from each scene when your two protagonists *have different attitudes* yet are involved in *the same line of action.*

If you are interested in writing a buddy picture, make certain that your two characters are emotionally and temperamentally, as well as physically, *different.* They must have different *attitudes.*

Ark Movies

There is a type of film story called the "ark" picture. These movies involve a group of people all caught in the same difficult circumstances. Among the earliest of these, and still one of the best, is Alfred Hitchcock's *Lifeboat* (John Steinbeck's story, Jo Swerling's screenplay). Here is a classic (literally) "We're all in the same boat" ark picture. Others crop up with some frequency during periods when Hollywood has a love affair with this type of movie: *Towering Inferno, Earthquake, The Poseidon Adventure*. A very early ark movie that was recently revived as an award-winning Broadway musical was *Grand Hotel.*

All of Hollywood's love affairs are short-lived and, at present, the ark movie is rare. As soon as somebody makes one that is a huge hit, however, dozens of others will follow. Example: *Alien* (co-written by Dan O'Bannon) is an ark movie that was quickly followed by *Aliens* and *Alien 3*. (We're all in the same spaceship.)

An excellent ark movie is *The Waterdance*, the story of a group of paraplegics in a rehab ward trying to cope with life confined to a wheelchair. Check it out.

Making a Scene

A scene has only one function, but that one is vital. *It is to deepen the readers' (audience's) involvement in your story and characters*. In a word, to keep them hooked.

You can accomplish this in many ways. The best way is to make certain that you are moving your story forward and not merely marking time. The first principle in writing a scene is identical to the first principle in writing the *first scene* of your screenplay: Your point of attack on each of your scenes should be the point at which *nothing need come before*. It is invariably a point of immediate and compelling interest.

Your job is to give your best effort to prevent lazy readers from taking the easy way out. Remember, you are generally dealing with readers who have the attention span of a gnat. Many of them don't want to like your screenplay. It makes work for them; they have to start phoning people, "take" meetings, start generating action, start a process that might result in nothing more than a lot of phone calls, and a lot of meetings. It is far easier to just toss your script aside with all the other rejects and move on to the next one. It's a sad reality in Hollywood.

The paradox is that everybody in the movie business loves a great scene; they will tell their friends about it, they will imagine selling it in a pitch meeting, they will imagine playing it, directing it, even imagine the audience's reaction to it, and, yes, even the Academy Award that may grow out of it.

So all is not lost; you are simply dealing with the fundamental love-hate relationship everybody in Hollywood has with a really good screenplay.

Location

As you approach a scene, take time to explore where you want to locate it. Try to avoid static locations such as offices, hotel rooms, park benches—any place where you are apt to have two or more characters sitting around talking to each other. That's called a "set piece." Nothing has more possibility to be boring. If, on the other hand, the scene *must* be played in a room, make certain it has a strong emotional dynamic, that something *important* is being talked about, and that there is tension or conflict between the talkers. You are almost always better off if your scene is located *outside* in an interesting location, with things happening in the background and all around the talkers. Keeping the characters moving helps. Movies are about *moving pictures*. Keep it in mind.

The greatest problem the adapter of a theatrical play has in turning a play into a movie is avoiding the confining three walls of the stage or, as we say, in "opening it up."

Even if you're writing an original, your job is still to "open it up." To bring maximum *visual interest* to the scene. Contrary to the misguided notion of certain film critics, it is the *screenwriter* who places the scenes in fascinating locations that will excite the eye as well as the ear. The director's job is to film those locations. James Bond movie stories were only fully developed *after* the locations were discovered, not before, and those melodramas were often more exciting for their locations than for their stories and characters.

It is always a good idea to find a location for your scene that will provide visual irony, such as two killers plotting their crime in a nursery school or doctors talking about their sex lives over an operation in progress.

What works best in scenes is what works best in stories—a strong element of surprise.

Most screenwriters spend as much time thinking about the right location to place a scene as on the content of the scene. It's always time well spent.

Rule of thumb: In building your scene, *do not tell us where we have been or where we are going next.*

Avoid either show-and-then-tell or tell-and-then-show; *both should be simultaneous.*

Avoid entrances and exits unless they increase audience (reader) interest in your story.

The Goal

Scenes will play and write better if each character in each scene has a *single goal or purpose* for this particular scene. This will provide you with the needed dynamics to make the scene come alive, and it will also provide you with the essential attitudes necessary to make a scene work.

Attitude

In approaching a scene, make certain you have fixed in your mind the *attitude* of every character in the scene. Every character must have an attitude to make the scene play. Otherwise, it will lie there like a dead mackerel. An actor cannot play a scene as a character who has no attitude. What is the character's *feeling* about what is happening in the scene? What does each character *want* in each given scene? There are no bystanders in screenplays, other than the extras who are in the background and are not a part of the story. Beware of placing passive characters in any scene; they can kill it.

Sub-Text

It is important to look for the sub-text in every scene—
what's *really* going on as opposed to what *appears* to be
going on. Sub-text adds depth and meaning to a scene
that might otherwise be meaningless and superficial. Sub-
text is parodied by Woody Allen in his outstanding comedy *Annie Hall.* Allen and Annie are on the rooftop of his
apartment building having a trivial boy-meets-girl introductory conversation, bland, innocuous. They are talking
about mundane matters, but the sub-titles on the screen
tell us what they are *thinking*: What sex together would
be like. It's an hilarious scene. It's also a superb lesson in
sub-text and is but one example of the originality of
America's foremost *auteur,* a writer who not only stars in
some of his own movies but directs them as well. Some
of Woody Allen's early movies are as good a course in
screenwriting as you are apt to find (that is until he
decided to reinvent himself as Ingmar Bergman). Like all
innovators, he can sometimes strike out, but like any true
artist, he allows himself the freedom to fail. Trial and
error is at the heart of all artistry.

Plotting

Now that you've got a fascinating protagonist, a line of action, and an opposing force, you are all set to plot your screenplay. Plotting is not the story but the *way* you decide to tell your story.

Plotting is the arrangement of the scenes (events). Most movie stories are told in a straightforward, sequential way. But more and more modern movie stories are told in non-linear ways. The purpose of this non-sequential storytelling style is to increase the dramatic impact of the story and to ensure that there will be as many surprising moments in the movie as possible.

Surprise, the *unexpected*, is the single most important weapon the screenwriter has at his or her disposal. It is vitally important in order to hold a modern audience or reader. When you realize that, thanks to television, almost everybody in America today has seen many *thousands* of movies in their lifetime, you begin to understand how difficult it is to create surprise and to overcome boredom. American movie audiences are increasingly sophisticated and reach a level of boredom remarkably quickly. American screenwriters and directors are intuitively aware of this and that is, no doubt, why they go to such lengths to create surprise and sustain dramatic tension.

I give my students one rule of thumb regarding the selection of scenes for their screenplay: *If you've seen it before, don't write it.* This is not so big a burden as it may

seem at first glance. Writers are growing more sophisticated, too. My students sometimes amaze me with their
ingenuity.

Creating new and fresh scenes is one of the most
important aspects of becoming a successful screenwriter.
For this reason, I have lost my infatuation with Syd Field's
paradigm.

Writing by the Numbers?

For the uninitiated, Field tells us that after reading
more than 2,000 screenplays over a two-year period, he
has been able to break down their structure as follows:
Act I is approximately page one to page thirty, Act II is
page 30 to page 90, Act III is page 90 to page 120. Field
also has a formula for developing characters involving
both the "Interior" and the "Exterior" of the characters. If
you like formulas, buy Syd's book *Screenplay*. It will help
some writers and hinder others.

During my early years of teaching screenwriting at
UCLA, I assigned Field's book to my students and asked
them for book reports to decide if I should advise the
campus bookstore to stock it for my classes. The student-
writer response surprised me. Most of them did not recommend Field's work; they wrote that it was too formulaic,
too cut-and-dried. Only a small minority vowed to use his
formulas in their work. I have no way of knowing if the
Field adherents fared better in the marketplace than those
who rejected the formulas. But my own conclusions are
clear. It is *not* valuable to recommend that new screenwriters write by the numbers.

I think after-the-fact analysis of screenplays might serve
a purpose for academicians, worried executives, nervous
producers, etc., but it will not, in and of itself, produce an
exciting and saleable screenplay. All art is, by definition,
a creative endeavor involving exploration, trial and error,

and, most important of all, the freedom to fail. There is no error-proof method for writing, painting, composing, creating dance, or living your life. Life and art would be unbearably dull if we were not free to explore, to challenge, to strike off on new journeys, to make daring choices. The essence of the first freedom for all creative people is *the freedom to fail.*

That good-intentioned people would come along with ideas to save creative folks from their follies is understandable. But where else in life can you experience the ultimate joy, yes, even the ecstasy, equal to those moments when your creative juices are flowing *freely?* You may strike out, it's true. But you will at least know you have been at bat and swung for the fences. (Babe Ruth was a great home-run hitter. He was also a strike-out king. It comes with the territory.)

I know Syd Field and respect him; we served on the Writers Guild Academic Liaison Committee together, and I think his contribution to understanding story structure is an important one. But, like all formulas, his tends to wear itself out with repeated use.

The great American movies usually defy formula writing.

As my good friend and movie critic Roger Ebert has written about *Citizen Kane:* "One of the reasons the film always seems fresh is that we never know what's coming next; the film has such an unpredictable structure . . . I have seen *Kane* at least thirty times and yet, when I walk in on the middle of a screening, or start my tape at random, I am unable to remember for sure what will come next."

I attended a seminar on "Film & Literature" in Key West this past winter. One of the panelists remarked, surprisingly, that all movie stories are told in three acts, to which fellow-panelist screenwriter William Goldman replied wryly, "Really? I didn't know that." I began to think of three of Goldman's best screenplays: *Marathon Man* (based on his novel), *A Bridge Too Far*, and *Butch Cassidy and the Sundance Kid.* None of them follow the conventional three-act structure. Yet I imagine a paradigm purist can come along and prove conclusively that these screenplays follow Syd Field's paradigm. Analysis of any art always finds what it is looking for. If you base screenplay analysis on the number and progression of "Acts," your critique will be based on the number and progression of "Acts." The reality is that there are no clearly defined "Acts" in screenplays. An "Act" is wherever you choose to say it is.

Can you imagine Orson Welles and Herman Mankiewicz sitting down to write and saying, "We've got to put Kane's announcement of his upcoming marriage on page . . ." 35 or 25 or 65? Do screenwriters really work that way? Perhaps a very few do; and probably more do so since Field's book came along. The results are a lot of formula-written movies that look and feel alike.

In my early teaching years, I could see value in the paradigm because it was, at that time, a fresh analysis of screenplay writing. However, as the years rolled on, I began to see a sameness in the story structure of too many screenplays and, not coincidentally, fewer and fewer fresh approaches and exciting new ideas. And, no fault of Field's, I'm sure, but more and more of my students were focusing on the quick sale, the hope for overnight screenwriting stardom—and the attendant big bucks— than were focusing on creating a great movie.

Another troubling aspect of laying out a formula for new writers is that they easily become slaves to it in their eagerness to jump-start their careers. I think the best way you can jump-start your career is to write a fresh and exciting screenplay nobody has seen before. Take off the straight jacket, which I know Field did not intend it to be. The bottom line is: When you structure your movie, *there is no one-size-fits-all.*

Check out *Dead Again*, a dazzling melodrama starring and directed by Kenneth Branagh (screenplay by A. Scott Frank). It is a lesson in non-linear storytelling while maximizing dramatic tension. Branagh, obviously a disciple of Orson Welles, nonetheless struck out on his own to create exciting mystery-movie pyrotechnics. This movie improves with each viewing.

Sequencing

Many top-drawer professional screenwriters today speak of their screenplay in terms of *sequences* or sections. Each sequence is an important phase of the story development and uses only as many scenes or pages as are needed to complete that particular section of the script. Each sequence should blend seamlessly into the next sequence. Each sequence continues the line of action, building toward the climax. It should all come together with as much fluidity as a symphonic tone poem, without stops and starts for individual movements. It seems to me that great music and great movies have much in common. Both are, at root, *theatrical* experiences, both weave and flow seamlessly through themes and varying tempos while building to dramatic climaxes and quiet resolutions. Every serious composer I have known and worked with over the years certainly had a keen sense of maintaining flow as well as *tension* in their compositions for dramatic films. If we focus our attention on sequences of events, we can give each the concentration it deserves as we simultaneously build to our climax.

Some screenwriters think ten major sequences are enough for a feature-length film, but it obviously depends upon the particular story. There is no set number for either scenes or sequences. Let's create an example of sequence.

Opening sequence: Jim and Linda have decided their marriage is finished and a divorce is necessary. Jim goes to a friend's law firm, where he meets divorce-attorney specialist Christine. That's a sequence: Getting the divorce underway.

Next sequence: Jim and Christine begin an impassioned affair while she tries to negotiate an "amicable" settlement with Linda's attorney (who is Christine's former lover). That's a sequence of an unknown number of scenes that will only be discovered in the writing.

As you're laying out the scenes in this sequence, try to make as many story-leaps as possible.

Story Leaps

By story-leaps, I mean skipping over any scenes that are not absolutely necessary to the presentation of your story.

Story-leaps work because of the sophistication of modern movie audiences, who will readily fill in the blanks for you. In truth, modern moviegoers are annoyed when you show or tell them something they have already figured out for themselves. Trust your audiences; they are not as dumb as the cynics would have you believe. They *want to become part of the storytelling process.* They don't mind a little mental work along the way. It is far better than being belittled by filmmakers who insist upon producing down to what they surmise to be audience stupidity. In the final analysis, the audience will always tell you if you've failed or not. That's why films are previewed.

Let's return to the sequencing of Jim and Linda's story.

The first story-leap is to *begin at the beginning* of an event. Jim and Linda are planning a calm, rational, amicable divorce. No scenes are necessary to "set up" the failure of the marriage. That's not our story. Ours begins with the amicable agreement to divorce. The theme of this story is that there is no such thing as a totally amicable divorce; the pain is just too great. But it is important that Jim and Linda think all will go smoothly. After all, they are two sophisticated, rational people, and this is the second marriage for both.

Next sequence: Linda learns of Jim's affair with his lawyer, and Linda is told by *her* lawyer what a real bitch Jim's lover-lawyer actually is. He does not mention their former affair. Linda gets steamed and turns down the settlement offer she has verbally agreed to. Jim responds in kind. That's a sequence of several scenes.

If you are critical about plotting your story, you will be surprised by how many unnecessary scenes you probably have included in each sequence. Story-leaps are a modern kind of shorthand that show respect for the intelligence of your audience. Never tell/show them *what they don't need to know.* Never tell/show them *what they can reasonably assume has happened. The last thing in the world you want is for your audience to get ahead of you.* Avoid this trap by being sharply critical of your scene selection. They key question is: *"Do I really need this scene?"* If in doubt, drop it. Your story is your master, not your scene. Don't sacrifice the big goal for the little moment.

After you've placed all your scene cards (more on this later) on the table, or the floor, or wherever and are studying your story, ask yourself: "Do I need the first ten or fifteen scenes?" The chances are, you don't.

To Outline or Not to Outline?

The only true answer to questions of story structure is that every screenwriter goes about structuring his or her story by their *instincts for the dramatic values in the story.* There is no better way.

Many top-level screenwriters I have known, worked with, or interviewed tell me they write from *no outline whatsoever.* I.A.L. Diamond (co-screenwriter with Billy Wilder on *Some Like It Hot, The Apartment, Irma La Douce,* and many others) told me he merely jots down some key story points on scraps of paper (sometimes brown paper bags from the market) and then goes to work on his screenplay. William Bowers (*The Gunfighter, The Sheepman, Support Your Local Sheriff,* etc.) started work on his screenplays by making a huge pot of coffee, putting a fresh, open pack of cigarettes on his desk top, gathering a handful of freshly sharpened Ticonderoga #2 pencils, and propping his feet up on his desk with a yellow lined, legal-sized notepad in his lap. Then he began *writing.* He liked to start with a character who was on his way to somewhere and to whom things kept happening to keep him from getting where he was going. I believe Bill knew what kind of things would be happening to his protagonist, and that's about all he needed to know to start writing. I doubt if he ever did a story outline in his life, except, possibly, in his head, or during the days when you could sell a "treatment." Those days are long gone. Now people only will buy, or even read, complete screenplays.

An outline may be helpful but most certainly is not necessary for *all* screenwriters. Again, the *no* one-size-fits-all guideline applies. Writing styles and methods vary as widely as the personalities of the writers—no two are alike. Find the method that is most comfortable and productive for you and stick with it. Your best teacher is always going to be yourself. Will you demand the best of yourself or will you settle for less? This is the determining factor for all writers, new or old, male or female, short or tall, lean or fat, black, white, yellow, brown, or purple.

The best way to tell your story is the way the story itself dictates. *Do not try to contort it into a predetermined form.* Movie stories have a way of imposing their own demands on the writer, just as the characters make their own demands. Listen to your characters and your story— both are right more often than any predetermined formula you may come up with.

Scene Cards

Many screenwriters, and not a few directors, lay out the movie they are going to work on on four-by-six-inch, lined index cards. One scene per card. Use a heavy pen and block lettering so that your notes are clearly visible from a distance. The great advantage of plotting your story on "scene cards" is the enormous flexibility it gives you. You can shuffle your scenes, literally, like a deck of cards, looking for the most effective way to tell your story. Best of all, you can lay out your cards on your dining-room table, coffee table, floor, bulletin board, sidewalk—any flat surface—and study how they look as a movie. If a scene seems out of place, remove that card and save it for possible later use or throw it away. You always have the movie *in its entirety* in this highly visible and flexible form. Changes are easy, require no typing or retyping, and you can always add a scene or take out a scene without disrupting the flow of the entire outline.

Here is an example of a scene card:

EXT. GYM-NIGHT   —10—
Ben tells Gayle to put
out or Get out of his
Company. Gayle says
take the Job and shove it
And Drives off.

Walter Newman uses scene cards like note pads, jotting down possible character names, bits of business, anything that he might want to later add into the screenplay. When he starts to write, he often has as many as 300 scene cards stacked beside his typewriter. (For easier visibility and less glare, Walter uses light blue cards.)

At this early juncture of laying out your story structure, you can help yourself enormously if you will heed the advice of screenwriter Anna Hamilton Phelan (*Gorillas in the Mist, Mask, Into the Homeland*). Anna says, "Write with no attachment to outcome."

In other words, let your ideas flow freely, remove all thoughts that come between you and your characters and/or your story. As you get in touch with your unconscious (where all creativity lies), you will unearth some new and richly rewarding ideas that will never enter your mind if you remain on the surface of your thinking. "Write with no attachment to outcome." Let the story and the people go wherever they want to take you. Now is the time to improvise, to get *your* conscious will out of it. You will now be tapped directly into your Muse, your unconscious. And you will be surprised at the treasures that lie waiting for you there.

As you think of a scene, jot down only the key action of the scene on a single card. Include only the major characters involved in the scene and no description of the setting unless it is so special that you feel you might otherwise forget it. Number the upper right-hand corner of the scene card *lightly*. You will probably be changing the scene sequence many times during this plotting process. It will take you sixty or more scenes before you have enough for a full-length (120-page) screenplay.

Lay out your scene cards anywhere you can stand and walk around them. You will find as you now analyze your movie that some of the scenes don't work, are unnecessary, or out of place. There will be countless revisions. The important thing is that you keep it flexible, keep the movie flowing with no "soft" spots, no sections that are merely filler waiting for the big scenes, the key scenes, to happen. No matter how long you spend sorting and shuffling your scene cards, you will find it time well spent.

In this shuffling and pruning process, the criteria for a scene are: Does it (1) advance the story, (2) increase the dramatic tension, (3) deepen our interest in the story and/or the character, or (4) create laughter? Every scene should meet at least one of these four requirements. Of the four, the most important is (2) increase the dramatic tension. Without tension, your reader has gone to sleep or tossed the screenplay aside.

Anna Hamilton Phelan has an interesting variation on the scene-card method of outlining. She lays out her story structure on a large roll of thick butcher paper, writing her scene notes with a large pen or crayon. This way she can unroll the paper across her office wall as she works and readily visualize the movie as it plays out. Anna takes her rolled outline to studio meetings, where she can display the proposed movie across the conference-room table and talk about it as the executives walk along the scroll that unrolls like a film being exhibited to the accompaniment of her narration. That's the way Anna sold her new and brilliant screenplay *Chains*. (Watch for *Chains*; it's a world-class screenplay.)

Some directors use scene cards when blocking out their approach to shooting the movie or diagnosing the story. Many editors also lay out the movie on scene cards, pinning them to the walls of their editing rooms to make certain that they have the proper sequence of events.

When debating whether or not to use this method or follow a predetermined paradigm, keep in mind that many movies are restructured in the editing room after shooting. The director's and the editor's purpose is the same as yours: To hold the audience.

Another advantage of the scene-card method is that it allows you, upon looking over your initial concept of a linear form of storytelling, to change your mind to a non-linear concept of flashbacks and/or flash-forwards, or to any variation you wish, and *see how it plays immediately* by merely reordering or replacing a few scene cards.

I use a large Marks-A-Lot pen to make my scenes easily visible as I walk around the table or lay them out on my office floor. And what of using colored cards? Some writers (and some directors) use colored cards to denote "high" scenes, key-action or story-point scenes, key emotional highs. This way, as you study your movie spread out before you, you can easily recognize the spacing of the high scenes and make sure they are spaced to achieve the maximum attention that you are after.

After you have the scenes you need to tell your story, you can decide if you want to use the Syd Field paradigm. However, the idea that *all* screenplays are written in three "acts" is nonsense. The truth is many screenplays use *five* acts, six acts, two acts, or any number of large, developmental story sections. There is no law in theatre or in film that says every drama must be told in three acts, even though that is the most frequently used form. Avoid rigidity, it is the death of creativity.

I believe that most screenwriters work like Jeffrey Boam.

> Froug: Do you follow a paradigm? Do you say, "Somewhere between page twenty and twenty-five, I've gotta have a first-act curtain"?
> Boam: No, not at all. I've got no rules, no guidelines to use. It's all pretty instinctive. . . . the biggest and most helpful rule I have is, when I'm bored, the screenplay is boring. And it's going to be boring for an audience.

After-the-fact analysis is, by definition, a study of what *was* done. *How* it was done is the essence of the creative process, which is a mystery too complex and too variable, writer-by-writer, to lay out as a how-to formula.

If you decide to use the scene-card method and you are fully satisfied with the way you have plotted your story, stack the cards in a pile on your desk and begin writing, scene by scene.

This is so important that I am going to repeat it: Once you start writing your screenplay, the most important advice I can possibly give you is to *keep going*. Do *not* go back and make revisions *under any circumstances*. Make notes in the margins of your pages, if you like, for future revisions, *but do not even think about those revisions until your first draft of the screenplay is completed*.

Once you go back to make any revision while you are pressing forward on the writing, you will never stop revising—you will be revising and revising behind yourself so often that you will find yourself writing in circles, and eventually you will throw away your screenplay in disgust. Once started, *press on* like there's a pack of wolves nipping at your ass.

A Movie Metaphor

A movie story is not a straight line hanging taut between two poles, like a clothesline on which you can hang scenes. That's the line of action. The story itself, and this is vital to keep in mind while plotting and writing, is a powerful river (to paraphrase Tolstoy): it curves around bends, surges through narrows, tumbles over rapids, here broad, calm but still powerful. The line of action and the opposing forces are the currents that keep the river always moving forward, in spite of cross-currents, toward its destination even as its course and forces change. This movie-story river has tributaries and channels that are offshoots of the main course (which are the sub-plots), but they do not halt the main current, which will, despite all obstacles, press forward to its destination. Movie stories *move* and *flow* with a kind of inevitability that sweeps us along, sometimes in spite of ourselves.

What It's About

Now you've got a story you're enthusiastic about and you feel you're ready to write the screenplay. Ask yourself a most important question before your begin: What is it about? I do not mean the plot, the arrangement of events, or even the characters. I don't mean *who* it's about, but *what* it's about. What are you saying in this story? What is your *point of view?* What is there about this story that engaged your heart and mind? What do you *feel* this story has to say? Where is *your* source of energy coming from as opposed to the story's source of energy?

When you have the answers to these questions, you have your *theme*. A theme is simply a proposition leading to a conclusion. Some call the theme a premise or a thesis. It does not matter what you call it, but you cannot write an outstanding screenplay without knowing what it is about. Usually, the theme is what has drawn you to the story in the first place, *even though you may not know it.*

Themes are sometimes pesky things; they like to hide behind the glitz and glamour of exciting events and characters. You must work your way deep into your story until you discover what it's about. Surprisingly, many screenwriters complete their screenplays without ever knowing what they're about. The result is, almost invariably, an empty and unsuccessful piece of work.

Examine great movies and you will always find the

theme readily apparent *and understandable* to almost everyone.

In *Home Alone*, John Hughes' comedy hit, the protagonist, an eight-year-old boy, is inadvertently left at home, alone, while his entire family goes to Paris for the Christmas holidays. He is confronted with two burglars attempting to break into his home. His cunning plan to outwit the thieves is what generates the line of action, counter-action, and hilarious audience response. As the clock in his home chimes nine o'clock, indicating the time the burglars will arrive, our young hero goes into action, but not before turning full-face to the camera and announcing: "It's my house. I have to defend it."

There it is, right at you—the theme of the movie. A man's (even a small boy's) home is his castle. It is what the movie is about and, as is usually the case with exceptionally popular movies, everybody can relate to it.

Another megahit movie, and one of the most popular ever made, is *E.T.* As almost everyone who has ever been to the movies knows, the theme of this film is: Home is where safety and security lie. This is a simple story by screenwriter Melissa Mathison, but it works miraculously well, in part, because everybody in the audience can relate to its theme.

There is nothing complicated about most movie themes. They are often based on simple homilies. Truisms that are, by definition, true. It seems not to matter in the least how trite or bromidic they are; in fact, it may be helpful to the success of the movie.

Rain Man was powered by a theme from the Bible: Am I my brother's keeper? Yes, you are, says Ron Bass' screenplay. Bass says the theme is actually a bit broader. He says it's about how difficult it is for us to relate to each other. But, he says, we *must* relate to be complete human beings.

There is more than one theme in a good movie; there are often many minor themes running concurrently, *but there is only one major theme.*

Think of your favorite symphonies, often richly textured works with many minor themes but almost always with one dominant theme that recurs and unites the work. So it is with great screenplays.

Here are some examples:

Dances with Wolves, an Oscar-winning film written by Michael Blake, based on his own novel, sets up the Native Americans as the good guys who teach a renegade cavalry officer (Kevin Costner) the need for harmony with nature and with each other. This idealized look at the first Americans is fairly dripping with brotherly love, yet, in spite of its sentimentality (maybe, in fact, because of it), it works. You can't beat brotherly love as a theme. We all must love each other. Anybody want to argue with that?

Spike Lee's *Do the Right Thing* ends with mixed messages: one is a quotation urging African-Americans to become militants, and the other quotation urges them to work for peaceful co-existence. Lee's Academy Award-nominated screenplay is richly textured and complex yet, in spite of his double messages at the end of the movie, a clear and unambiguous theme comes through loud and clear. "Are we going to love each other or what?" asks Lee's disc jockey narrator in the aftermath of onscreen violence. And that, more than any tacked-on quotations at the film's end, is clearly Spike Lee's theme and his message. *We must learn to love each other.* Unless we love each other, violence and destruction will follow.

Citizen Kane's major theme is clearly Lord Acton's dictum: "Power tends to corrupt, absolute power corrupts absolutely."

Fatal Attraction tapped into William Congreve's assertion of the late 17th century: "Heaven has no rage like love to hatred turned, nor hell a fury like a woman scorned." A more contemporary expression of this might be: Beware of one-night stands, there could be Hell to pay.

The main theme of *Gone With The Wind* is also Scarlett O'Hara's personal theme, "Strength of will, character, and determination will overcome any obstacle." In Scarlett's case, the focus of that determination is getting back to her roots, to home, to Tara. Show me a character with monumental grit and a nothing-will-stand-in-my-way attitude and I will show you the stuff of great movies.

The major theme is the heart and soul of your screenplay. Without a theme, your script will be hollow, empty. Study the themes of each movie you see, the minor themes as well as the major theme.

Characters have themes, too, and sometimes they are not the same as the theme of the story. A case in point is David Mamet's *The Untouchables*, the theme of which, in its final and most simplistic form, is the traditional "Crime does not pay." The theme of the protagonist, Treasury Agent Eliot Ness (Kevin Costner), however, is that in order to bring criminals to justice, you may have to break the law. Mamet's screenplay is a fresh look at the old, familiar story of Thirties Chicago ganglord Al Capone. Mamet proves yet again that an old story becomes a new story when told in a new way. Even though *The Untouchables* had been a long-running and highly successful television series, Mamet's movie attracted large audiences because it was a new and fresh look. Old stories never die, they often merely improve with the retelling.

I was moderator for a screenwriting panel at Sherwood Oaks Experimental College some years ago, and among the panelists of outstanding screenwriters was one of the greatest, Frank Pierson (*Cat Ballou, Presumed Innocent, In Country, A Star is Born, Cool Hand Luke*). He told an important story about the need to find a theme or "take" on your protagonist before you write your screenplay. Frank had accepted a contract to write what he later titled *Dog Day Afternoon.* It's the true story of a bank robber who held a large number of bank employees hostage while he negotiated with the police for money and a plane to take his homosexual lover to Sweden for a sex-change operation. Meantime, the bank had been surrounded by the police, and thousands of spectators were watching events unfold live and on television. It became a media circus.

Frank came to regret taking the assignment. He simply could not figure out what his protagonist was all about. While trapped in the bank along with his hostages, John Cazale (Frank's fictional name for the real-life robber) did everything he could to make his hostages comfortable. He served them coffee, brought them chairs, constantly assured them that they would not be harmed, and was exceedingly polite in an odd way for a man holding hostages at gunpoint. Frank knew that without a theme or take on his protagonist he could not write a scene. He told us he paced the beach, searching for an answer for weeks, trying to figure out what his story was about. He decided it would be no help to interview the actual robber now in a federal penitentiary. "Cazale wouldn't know either," said Frank.

Searching into the depths of meaning of his protagonist's behavior, Frank finally found the answer. John Cazale was caught in his own web of self-destruction. Cazale was a seemingly happily married man with children; he was also desperately trying to help his homosexual lover, who had urged him to get the money for the sex-change operation. Cazale, Frank decided, was a man trying to do the impossible: he wanted to make everybody happy in all circumstances. "He was trying to be a magician," Frank told us. "When I understood that, I could write the screenplay."

The theme of this excellent movie is, If you try to please all the people all the time, you are doomed to failure.

Frank's screenplay won him an Academy Award.

See *Dog Day Afternoon* and study the work of an outstanding screenwriter.

The late Hollywood mogul Samuel Goldwyn was quoted as saying to his screenwriters, "If you want to send a message, call Western Union."

But the blunt truth is, *every movie has a "message,"* and the screenwriter is the person who decides what that message is. It is the theme.

You can "discover" your theme as you are writing, but you are much better off knowing it *before* you start to write. When you have the theme going in, you also have the conclusion of the movie. It is the conclusion your proposition led you to.

The following story illustrates the strength a powerful theme gives you as you are writing.

When *Casablanca* was being filmed, there was indecision about the ending. According to Aljean Harmetz's well-researched history of the making of *Casablanca*, *Round Up the Usual Suspects*, the ending of the movie was rewritten many times during its shooting but none of the alternate endings was actually filmed. All versions protected the central theme: Bogart makes a commitment to join the fight against the Nazis. As always, the *details* of how you end your screenplay are not critical *as long as you protect your theme.*

The truth is, any version of the ending would have worked because *all were validations of the theme.* The theme of *Casablanca* is: In the center of warring factions, you can not remain neutral. Throughout the movie, Humphrey Bogart is trying not to take sides between the Nazis and the Free French. Julie Epstein and his brother, Phillip, along with Howard Koch, moved Rick (Bogart) from neutrality and cynicism to commitment, thus proving their premise. It did not weaken the theme if Bogart kept Bergman for himself or sent her away; he was now committed to the cause of freedom.

The movie has become, with the acid test of time, one of the most satisfying films ever made, aided by a superb and enduring theme.

The theme does not have to be announced to the audience. Most often, it is something the audience *senses* and, if they liked the movie, will discuss later.

There is not a standard placement for the theme, even though it most frequently shows up at the conclusion of the movie.

In the early days of the movies, during the era of Hollywood's establishment of its first self-censorship code under the leadership of Will Hays, all crime melodramas, by edict, had to have the same theme: Crime does not pay. Today, in our more enlightened era, we have plenty of crime melodramas proving the premise that sometimes crime *does* pay.

In *Butch Cassidy and the Sundance Kid,* William Goldman states his theme (the proposition) in the first scene: The West is changing, growing sophisticated. The old western outlaws are on their way out. In the last scene of the movie, he reveals the conclusion of his theme: You must change with the times or die. Having a clear point of view about his two characters and what they represented is an important reason why Goldman was able to write this highly successful screenplay.

Check out the theme of every movie you see. Sometimes a character will state the theme. Example: In Lawrence Kasdan's crime melodrama *Body Heat,* a friend says to the protagonist, Ned Racine (William Hurt), "Ned, some day that prick of yours is going to get you into a whole lot of trouble." The truth, known to the audience but not the detective, is that Ned's sexual obsession with Matty (Kathleen Turner) has already gotten him involved in committing the murder of her husband. That is Kasdan's theme: Sexual obsession leads to self-destruction.

The theme of Larry Gelbart's and Murray Schisgal's excellent comedy *Tootsie* is stated by Dustin Hoffman to Jessica Lange in the last scene of the movie. The theme is about men accepting the softer, more feminine aspects of their masculinity. Perhaps the theme might be broadened to suggest that we would all be better off if, no matter which gender we are, we understood that we must be kinder to one another.

When you look at movies that seemed, at least on the surface, to have everything but still left you feeling unsatisfied, you will almost always find that the problem is a lack of theme or point of view by the screenwriter. No matter how hard you have to dig, keep digging, find the meaning of the story, or, at least, the meaning *to you.* Without it, your screenplay will be hollow.

Unless you have a clear-cut point of view about the movie you are writing, you will not write a good movie.

Writing
the
Script

In preparation for your screenwriting endeavors, I hope you have read as many screenplays as you can find, preferably *not* those published in book form.

It is important to know that published screenplays are not in the form the writer submitted. Screenwriters write in Master Scenes, using camera angles *only when they are essential to heightening the dramatic tension.* Published screenplays will probably indicate many camera angles, which are frequently typed in by the production secretary or the studio typing pool (presently called Data Processing). This is to help the production departments, assistant director, unit production manager, et al., to lay out what's called a Day Out Of Days Shooting Schedule.

In this production version of the screenplay, scenes are numbered for their convenience. *Do not number the scenes of the screenplay you submit.* It immediately tells the professional reader that the writer is a novice. You may be a novice, but you don't need to advertise it.

Don't try to be "creative" with screenplay form, especially when numbering pages. Page numbers should *always be in the upper right hand corner of the page,* where every professional reader knows to find them. As they read screenplays, they keep tabs on the page number to see where they are in the movie. One minute per page is average playing time for a movie. However, this can vary as much as twenty or thirty minutes for a two hour film, depending upon the pace of the director.

Whatever you do, make the reading of your screenplay an *enjoyable* experience. You are not writing *The History of Time.*

Beginning the Writing

Stack your scene cards, if you choose to use them (or your notes or outline), on your desk beside your typewriter (or word processor) and peel them off the top as you write. However, it is most important that you feel the freedom to take off in new directions as the work progresses. New scene ideas will certainly occur to you. And your characters will sometimes insist on going in another direction. Go with them, explore. Something much more interesting might turn up. *Do not hesitate to follow your muse.* This is the real joy of writing; without it you become a slave to an outline. Don't let a sense of boredom creep into your work. *You are your most important audience.* Remember, *if you are bored, most certainly your reader will be bored.* And it follows that there will never be a film and thus never an audience.

Lest your muse take you too far afield, keep in mind your obligation to your line of action and your theme. If you wander too far from either, you might easily wind up writing in circles on an endless journey to nowhere.

It is most important that the writing of the screenplay be a richly rewarding experience, that you lose yourself in it, and that, finally, it takes over your life until you can hardly think about anything else. This happens to all of us. Sometimes it drives us a little crazy, and sometimes we find ourselves overjoyed by the things the characters are saying and doing.

Jeffrey Boam told me that in the midst of writing *Lethal Weapon III* he could not get the screenplay out of his mind, even as he and his wife attended other movies. "It nearly drove me crazy," he said. This is par for the course for all screenwriters. The goal of the writing process is to reach such a deep level of intimacy with your characters that they become totally separate from you, yet *totally* real. If you achieve this level of intimacy, you, like your audience, will wonder what surprising things your characters are going to do or say next.

Page One

The most important and the most difficult page any new screenwriter will ever write is page one.

The bald truth is that this page is your entrance into the world of professionals in the motion picture and/or television community.

In this very first page, any professional reader will get an immediate sense of the level of your writing. If your screenplay is at least professional *looking*, the chances are that the reader will read page one and move on to the next page. If it isn't, the ballgame is over.

You have about ten pages in which to grab a professional reader's attention. If you haven't hooked them by then, your script will, in all likelihood, be tossed onto the very tall stack of rejects.

You must remember that you are writing a script *to be read*, not a shooting script. *Do not, under any circumstances, write a shooting script*, even if you hope to direct it.

If your script is good enough, it will be read and read again by scores of professional people long before anybody decides to film it. Read William Goldman's screenplay for *Butch Cassidy and the Sundance Kid* to see how entertaining a movie script can be.

Great screenplays make for entertaining reading: The reader can see the movie on the page, even feel the excitement. There should be *very few* camera angles to clutter up the reading.

Agents will read the script. *If they like it*, actors, directors, producers, studio executives, and a small army of people will also read it. It will be read again and again and again before anybody says, "Yes, let's buy it, let's make it."

Opening Signal

The "let's buy it" possibility must take hold on page one of your screenplay.

Here is what page one must look like, what it must contain, and what it must do.

(1) It must be typed *perfectly*, error-free.

(2) It must be reader-friendly. Not only easy to read but enjoyable to read. The reader must be *drawn* to page two.

(3) Page one, line one, should tell the reader in unmistakable terms the *genre* of your movie. Is it a comedy? A mystery? A melodrama? A tragi-comedy? A flat-out drama? Make sure you tell your reader what they are in for on page one, how you expect them to react. This is the Opening Signal. Often, your indication of the kind of music you want will reveal the genre. Indicate the music you want at the heading of your first scene. (You may choose a title for your script that will indicate it's genre, though this is not necessary.)

(4) Focus on your protagonist *without using a camera angle*; show the reader *who* this story is going to be about.

(5) Do not write lengthy descriptions of locales or sets. A beach is a beach. Unless there are some striking features about this particular stretch of beach, nothing else about the location need be said. Keep the reader moving along, throw no obstacles in his or her path.

(6) Start your script with an *action* or an *event*. Most

movies start with an event:

- A death — *Citizen Kane* and countless others.
- An arrival — *Singin' in the Rain.*
- A departure — *Kramer vs. Kramer* — wife leaving her husband and their child.
- A burglary — how many countless melodramas have begun this way?
- A murder — a standard for television melodrama.
- A wedding — *The Godfather* is but one of countless films to begin this way.

(7) Page one need not be a full page, just enough to hook the reader and force him to turn to page two to *see what happens next.*

(8) A story must be underway on page one; *something is happening or about to happen.*

(9) Make it clean and quick. Hook the reader and move right along.

Here is an important, true story that illustrates the significance and necessity of the opening signal.

Bob Altman, director of the movie *M*A*S*H*, told me that at the preview screening of this movie, the audience sat in stony silence for the first twenty minutes of the film. Reacting to the opening shot of helicopters coming into the Mobile Army Surgical Hospital grounds loaded down with bloodied, badly wounded soldiers, members of the audience told themselves, It's a war movie, it's *serious*— laughter would be an inappropriate response. So, in spite of the movie's comedic elements, nobody laughed. They felt uncomfortable.

Bob says he went home that night discouraged; the audience totally misunderstood the movie. He told his concerns to his then-teenaged son Mike. "Not to worry," said the lad, "I've written the perfect lyrics for a song for your movie." The kid then recited his lyrics for "Suicide Is Painless." Bob says he rushed to the phone and called his old friend, composer Johnny Mandel. Johnny came up with a melody for young Altman's lyrics, and together they created the song that launched both the movie and the television series that followed. Bob hired a chorus to sing "Suicide is Painless" and placed the music track under the film's opening shot of helicopters arriving with their wounded troops. Audiences began laughing from the first frames forward and Bob had his megahit, generated by Ring Lardner Jr.'s Oscar-winning screenplay.

The next movie you see, note the time it takes you to recognize the opening signal. I can't over-stress its importance. It's the genre. Check every movie you see from this day forward.

The story is already underway on page one. Note the *event* that starts a movie in the first scene. Check it out in all the movies you see. Believe me, what's on the screen was *written in the screenplay.*

That's the *easy* part about writing page one. Let's get on to the most important and most difficult aspect of page one.

Point of Attack

The beginning is *that which nothing need come before and something must follow,* says Aristotle. Your story must not only be *underway* on page one, but the first scene must be the *immediate* and *only* way to start your movie. This is called the Point of Attack. You do not need to *set up* your protagonist first; your protagonist must "set up" himself or herself *by his or her behavior* and by the *circumstances in which we discover him or her.* Nothing more needs to be said. And you certainly do not need to "set up" the story; it is immediately happening before our very eyes as the movie opens.

In ninety percent of the student screenplays I have read, you could throw out the first ten or fifteen pages and improve the screenplay one hundred percent. New screenwriters are so anxious to prove themselves and the worthiness of their material that they will go to absurd lengths to tell the reader everything the reader does not need to know *before* the story begins. This is a critical point, but a hard one to convey to new screenwriters. Eagerness to please is certainly no crime, but it is often a recipe for self-destruction.

Once you start writing the screenplay, you have *two audiences* you must please—yourself and, in the process, your reader. Pleasing yourself, alone, is only a self-defeating form of masturbation. Slow starts can defeat you before you begin if you do not start your screenplay on a moment *nothing need come before.* Your point of attack explains itself; it does not need to "set up" anything.

Of all the poor excuses student screenwriters used to give me for dawdling around in the first ten or fifteen pages of the script, the weakest was, "I thought I had to set up the character." Whoever spread this ugly rumor among beginning screenwriters should be boiled in oil. When your reader reads *page one* of your screenplay, make certain he or she cannot resist turning to page two because *you have got him or her hooked.* This is what separates the professionals from the novices.

The chances are that you will spend more time thinking about your point of attack than any other aspect of your screenplay. Fine. It will be time well spent.

Writing a Scene

The current style is to make scenes brief, very brief. Say, half a page or even less. Thanks in part to MTV and TV commercials (shorthand shotgunning of information), readers and audiences alike now expect you to show your wares and get off, moving right along.

This is not to say *all* scenes *must* be short, only that most of them are in current screenplays.

A staccato pace is most effective in the genres of melodrama, comedy, and farce.

In drama and tragedy, where characters are more fully explored and events are more the clashes of inter-personal human dynamics rather than crashing cars and exploding bodies, you will need more than a half-page to develop your characters and your situations. Your readers will understand this since they will know your genre and what to expect from your opening signal.

Even though you have the relative luxury of time to more fully explore character and nuance in drama and tragedy, you still can't afford to dawdle. Figure about four pages is a good, average scene length in these genres. Television has had an enormous impact on movie audiences' attention spans. They are impatient, they are restless, just like the readers of your screenplay. Except the audience has paid to see your movie *and, unlike your readers, they want to like it.*

The one exception to moving your story forward with every scene: If you have a scene that is strikingly hilarious, you don't have to worry if it will advance your story or not. Everybody, readers and audiences alike, will happily take a pause for a good laugh. But do not drift too far from your line of action.

If you feel you must have a long conversational scene, break it up into several overlapping scenes. *Make certain there's dramatic tension in it.* Keep the dialogue continuous but shift locations as the characters explore what they must say. Work and rework the dialogue until you are *absolutely certain* you need all those words. More often than not, you don't. You will learn as you study movies that, in many cases, actors can say more with an exchange of glances than all your wordiness can convey. *Trust the actors.* I do not mean that you should trust them as writers—far from it. Trust them to deliver much more than you ever expected with their *first performance.* Like it or not, if you are determined to be a dramatist, actors will be your lifetime collaborators.

The Beginning

The avant-garde French director Jean-Luc Goddard once observed that every story has a beginning, a middle, and an end, but not necessarily in that order. It's a most accurate comment.

More and more movies today, thanks, in part, to pioneers like Goddard, juggle their story structure around in unpredictable ways to maximize the vital element of surprise and avoid the unforgivable sin of boredom. When you have completed your scene-card structure, I suggest that you lay out your projected movie on a flat surface and re-examine it to see if there is a more interesting, non-sequential way to tell your story. The only "rule" you need to follow is your sense of what will provide the greatest dramatic tension and yield the greatest dramatic impact.

I repeat, forget the notion of a one-size-fits-all formula. It will only assure you of being predictable and uninteresting.

Here are the elements you must have in the beginning section of your screenplay:

(1) You must introduce the protagonist and his or her problem.

(2) You must also define his or her *need*.

(3) You must show the *circumstances* and *situation* the protagonist lives with. This is done in the *first scene* where we meet him or her. A protagonist is immediately (though only partially) defined by the other characters with whom he or she associates—"We are known by the company we keep."

(4) You must introduce or foreshadow the *antagonist*, the opposing force, whether internal or external.

(5) You must establish the *line of action*.

(6) You must begin the path of *rising action*, by foreshadowing what sorts of troubles may lie ahead. This helps you start dramatic tension very early on. (Rising action is a term that indicates the increasing tension that you need as the story builds to its climax. It is the gradual turning of the screw.)

All of the above are best done through *behavior* rather than dialogue. Beware of expository dialogue, the curse of new screenwriters. Don't tell us where we're going or where we've been. Show-and-tell is not good screenwriting. Neither is tell-and-show. *They should be simultaneous.* Reveal only as much about your protagonist *as is absolutely necessary*. Information about important characters should always be *leaked out* on a *need-to-know* basis. What your audience does *not* know but *wants to know* is an excellent device to hold their attention. Remember Alfred Hitchcock's comment, "The person who tells you everything about themselves right away is a bore."

When you are reading William Goldman's screenplay for *Butch Cassidy and the Sundance Kid*, or seeing the film, note that you do not learn that Sundance was born in New Jersey until later in the film, after they have arrived in Bolivia. Nor do you learn that Butch has never killed a man until that moment in Bolivia when he *must* kill a man. Both these quite incidental but interesting facts about Goldman's protagonists are not revealed until the moment of *optimum dramatic effect.* Revealed earlier or in incidental dialogue, they would have been boring biographical filler.

Take great care in withholding fascinating background on your characters until it will add something to a dramatic moment. If there is no such moment, then don't tell us at all; obviously, we don't need it.

Because *you* are fascinated by some obscure aspects of your character's history does not mean that your reader will be. If in doubt, keep the information to yourself.

If your protagonist is fascinating, you can be sure your reader/audience will hang in there to find out what your story is about. If your protagonist is only mildly interesting, it doesn't matter one bit how much you tell the readers; they will have already tossed the screenplay aside.

Need to Know

You do not and should not explain everything right away. Like the characters, the meaning of the events happening in the screenplay *should reveal themselves.* Avoid the common fault of new screenwriters who often feel it is necessary to tell their reader and/or audience exactly what's going on. Ask yourself what *must they know* at this point in time in my story? If you tell them anything beyond this bare minimum, you will undercut your own story.

The function of the beginning is not merely to get the story underway, but to make absolutely certain you are holding your readers in rapt attention, eager to read on *to find out what happens next.*

The first writing I ever did was a mystery novella called *Enough Money*. Having no textbooks and no teachers aboard a subchaser off Einewetok Atoll in the Central Pacific during World War II, I had to find my own way as a storyteller. My solution was remarkably simple: I made up the story as I went along, never having any idea what was going to happen next. I assured myself of reader surprise because *I* was surprised every day by my own mystery. Each day as I pecked away on my Royal portable typewriter, I told myself a story. As soon as my tour of duty as the commanding officer of PC800 ended, I got my manuscript to an agent in New York, who sold it almost immediately, and my career as a professional writer was launched. I have never forgotten the value of letting your instincts guide you as you write.

A Non-Formula for Successful Screenwriting

When I interviewed I.A.L. Diamond for *The Screenwriter Looks at the Screenwriter*, I asked him, "What makes a great screenplay?" His reply is valuable to all aspiring screenwriters:

"Oh, god, I wish I knew, because I would put it in a sealed envelope and sell the secret. I don't know. Something you have to feel by instinct and experience, and then one time out of three, at least, you're wrong. I don't think anybody can give you a formula, or pinpoint it that well."

In light of that, it is important to point out Iz's response to my question: "How long do you allow yourself for the development of your story before you begin the screenplay?"

Diamond: ". . . oh, I may have been thinking about a thing on and off for months or even years. But when I actually get down to work, I will spend no more than two weeks beforehand, making notes. I'm afraid that if I get it worked out too well, then I'm going to find the writing boring. I'd rather just have a few signposts and leave a lot of wide-open spaces, so things can happen when I'm writing. I don't like to have it down too cold or too well figured out before I start, because I think some of the excitement and enthusiasm goes out of it."

Every screenwriter has his or her own unique method for writing and/or planning the screenplay. There is no *one way, no correct way.* There is only *your* way, and that is the best possible way you can find for yourself. It may take several drafts and several screenplays, but if you are patient and if you will grant yourself the freedom to fail, you will most certainly find your own style and that will, without question, be the right one for you. There are as many ways to attack the writing of the screenplay as there are writers.

Here's a comment from Daniel Pyne in response to my question "What makes a screenplay great?"

"Having a compelling story, well told in an interesting way, not by any formula. I completely eschew the formula of first, second, and third acts. I've run into too many writers who get lost in that old formula. They know where the first act ends, and they know where the second act ends, but their entire script is treading water because they're just writing from point to point."

If you keep the events happening and the dramatic tension increasing, you will never even pause to think of a formula or even "act breaks." You will be writing with a new found confidence.

If you find yourself getting bored during the writing, you will know with the certitude of your own gut instincts that it is time for you to create something new to happen, some new events, some new *problems*, something to strongly hold your reader's interest. You are never helpless as a writer. *You always have your all-powerful secret weapons: your instinct and your imagination.*

Back in the Sixties, I sold a movie treatment to Hollywood producer Walter Mirisch (*The Magnificent Seven, In the Heat of the Night, Hawaii, Same Time Next Year,* etc.) and was hired to write the screenplay and produce the movie. As I was working on the screenplay, Walter advised me, "Put your hero up a tree and keep throwing rocks at him."

Maybe that's not a formula for success as a dramatist and screenwriter. But William Shakespeare did it, so did Eugene O'Neill, so does Arthur Miller, so does Edward Albee and almost every screenwriter I ever met or worked with.

As my pal Bill Bowers once said to me, "Life is just one damned thing after another."

Dr. M. Scott Peck, the eminent psychiatrist/author/lecturer, begins his seminal work, *The Road Less Travelled,* with this sentence, "Life is difficult." All Drama is based on this simple truth.

Let's assume that you have everything perfectly set in motion in The Beginning and now you must move on. In order to do this, you merely add the complications, which we call The Middle . . .

The Middle

Aristotle says the middle is that which must follow something and something must follow it. You can't get more basic than that, and I am not foolish enough to try to top Aristotle.

The middle of your screenplay is the largest section of your script. It sometimes is called The Complications. I call it The What Goes Wrong. Unfortunately, a lot of modern movies fall apart because they have no middle, only a beginning and an end. This produces a story that seems thin and insubstantial.

I suggest that you do not think of the middle as Act Two. We are not playwrights, in spite of the similarities between our work. In film, there is no curtain, invisible or otherwise, that will go up or down at various points in our drama. True, we write drama, but after that the similarity becomes forced. I will not bore you with all the reasons screenwriters and playwrights are different animals. You've seen enough plays in theatres or on television to understand the difference yourself.

More and more screenwriters today are eschewing the old-fashioned credit that used to read "Screenplay by" and are now taking "Written by" as their credit when they have written both the story and the screenplay, which asserts film writers are *screenwriters*, not *play*wrights writing motion pictures. The disparity between the two professions widens as new generations of writers learn more and more new ways to use the film medium to tell their stories.

Thanks to new styles of movie storytelling, we do not need to think of The Middle as Act 2, 3, 4, 5, 6, or 7. Break away from theatre-drama thinking and bring yourself into the world of movie thinking, where so many things are happening in screenplays, and happening so fast to so many people in so many places that the old-fashioned notion of a curtain coming up or going down is irrelevant and only limits your thinking.

Think of writing the middle as a chess game in which you control both sides of the board. As the screenwriter, this is your rare chance for total objectivity, playing protagonist as well as antagonist. You make a move (as protagonist), your opponent (antagonist) makes a counter-move. You introduce *new and unexpected complications and problems*. And so it goes, move and counter-move, escalating the action and the stakes (the turning of the screw) until you feel you have reached a point of no return, until you are at the peak of the conflict and have arrived at the climax.

This is the process of creating a middle. Escalating and complicating dramatic tension until your instincts tell you that you have nowhere to go but to the final confrontation—your climax. There are no rules about this, only your gut instinct that will tell you enough is enough and the climax can no longer be delayed. Thrusts and counter-thrusts, actions and reactions, will inevitably take you to your climax. It is inescapable.

Study every movie you see and watch as the actions

and reactions escalate. Study the moves and counter-moves that force the story to a climax. Obviously, these moves and counter-moves vary widely with each story you tell. Your instinct will guide you, and you can sharpen that instinct by studying every movie you see.

Your middle is not only What Goes Wrong, but how you play the chess game.

You can see this chess game vividly illustrated in Jeffrey Boam's *Lethal Weapon III,* the megahit of the summer of '92. Jeff's action-adventure melodrama leaps from sequence to sequence, in a mind-spinning whirl of set-pieces. As the episodes escalate toward the final confrontation between the good guys (Mel Gibson and Danny Glover) and the villain, we are rocked from scene to scene with almost no transitions and most certainly no "act" breaks. This is melodramatic shorthand at its most effective level. It's the slam-bam school of screenwriting that is clearly the style of choice in current melodrama, which I would suggest we call comedy-melodrama (Jeff is proud to call himself a comedy writer), but is inappropriate in other genres.

In the 1992 Academy Award-winning *Silence of the Lambs,* you have a much more subdued style of melodrama, and yet it plays out as a series of progressive set-pieces. Clarice Starling (Jodie Foster), the young FBI agent, first meets convicted killer Dr. Hannibal Lecter (Anthony Hopkins) and is thwarted in her efforts to get information from him. Subsequent scenes between them build slowly in dramatic intensity as the story's deadline element is emphasized. Introducing a time-limit is a dramatic device as old as the movies and one that will, no doubt, be with us forever (though sometimes it does get a bit frayed at the edges). Putting a deadline in your story may help, but it will not salvage a weak story. The Western classic *High Noon* used the device to perfection.

A time-line, as in *Silence of the Lambs*, overrides and obviates any need for artificial act breaks in your thinking. The only guide you need as you write the middle of your screenplay is the one that has guided all dramatists since the ancient Greeks: *Escalate the dramatic tension.* No formula is needed to do this. The rest will take care of itself.

Shifting to straight drama: What is the middle of Arthur Miller's *Death of a Salesman* all about but the escalating conflict and dramatic tension resulting from Willy Loman's mental breakdown?

In John Singleton's superb *Boyz in the Hood*, what is the middle all about except the escalating of dramatic tension as the violence in the protagonist's neighborhood gangs edges ever closer to him and his friends? (To my mind, *Boyz* was the best original screenplay of 1991. Rent the video and you will see a superb example of classic contemporary drama.)

This is also true in the comedy genre. In *Tootsie*, the middle is all about everything that can go wrong does go wrong, and the conflict escalates.

No matter what the genre, from farce to tragedy, the middle is *always* about what goes wrong and *escalating dramatic tension*. It's a kind of Murphy's Law—"What can go wrong will go wrong." It is an obstacle course for your protagonist.

If you feel that your middle is sagging or that your story seems thin, the answer is to *create more problems for your characters*. If that means adding characters and/or another sub-plot, then by all means do so. The middle of your screenplay is not about cause and effect; it is about *causes and effects.*

Your complications are generated by two fundamental sources—what your characters *do* to further their goal and what is *done to them* because of their determination to pursue their goal. Both ideas must be at the center of your thinking as you begin to write the middle of your screenplay. There is no mystery in this. What does your protagonist *have to do* and who or what *gets in his or her way to make it extremely difficult?*

The answer to all writing problems can be found *inside your characters.* When I say that the answer lies inside your characters, I am also saying that the answer lies inside you. The characters are your creation—you know them better than anyone else ever will. You will find as you write and explore them that they are *your friends*, antagonists as well as protagonists. At times, they may frustrate you, but in the end, they will help you *if, by putting your ego aside, you let them.*

Of course, good structure is vital to all screenwriting (good structure simply means that which will escalate dramatic tension and thereby hold, and even escalate, reader/audience attention), but we must focus our attention on the *creative* rather than the mechanical aspects of writing screenplays. If the artistry is there, the structure can be readily adjusted; if the artistry is not there, no amount of tinkering with the structure will save it.

Screenwriters today have more creative freedom than they have ever known in the history of motion pictures, both in terms of subject matter as well as in style and manner of storytelling.

Thanks to the pioneering filmmakers of the Sixties

(especially the foreign filmmakers such as De Sica, Fellini, Godard, Truffaut, Bergman, Antonioni, Kurosawa, et al.— the makers of the post-World War II so-called "art films"), the old conventions of chronological, sequential, storytelling are frequently being replaced by non-linear time shifts—rapidly moving from the present to the past, from flash-forward to flashback, and again to the present without break or explanation. Sophisticated modern audiences can absorb these time shifts with ease as long as the base *line of action* moves forward at a strong and continuous pace. A recent, highly successful example of a screenwriter defying conventional form in order to maximize dramatic impact is Cynthia Cidre's superb screenplay *Mambo Kings*, based on Oscar Hijuelos' Pulitzer Prize-winning novel, *The Mambo Kings Play Songs of Love*. Ms. Cidre explores the two protagonists' (brothers) former lives and romances in their native Cuba without ever letting the present-time story lose a shred of its dramatic tension. This is an example of the kind of movie shorthand now available to screenwriters that would have been unthinkable only a few years ago.

If you don't use page numbers to signify "acts" or "turning points," how do you know if your screenplay is developing as strongly as you want it to?

Craft and Art

This question goes to the quintessential interaction between craft and art. Craft is important in the creation of all art forms, but craft alone is meaningless without artistry.

As a successful Hollywood television writer-producer and teacher for almost forty years, I was far more interested in writers whose work demonstrated promising artistry than in those who had the craft down cold.

My good friend Dan O'Bannon comes to mind. When Dan showed me his first screenplay, *The Devil in Mexico*, back in the early Seventies, I was astonished first by its length (over 200 pages) and then by the clumsiness of its structure and its scenes. It was clearly the work of a young, struggling novice.

But what a gifted novice Dan was! His protagonist (Ambrose Bierce) was one of the most original characters I had ever encountered in a screenplay. And the story (Bierce, as an old man going into Mexico to join Pancho Villa's revolutionary forces) was an original in the best sense of the word. The dialogue was all over the place— endless speeches, interspersed with dazzling interchanges between Bierce and Villa. Here was a writer to be reckoned with.

I took him to meet my business manager and attorney, and we discussed how best to launch Dan's career.

Alas, his script was in no shape to show an agent; Dan would have to write others until he united his undeniable artistry with a better understanding of the craft of screenwriting.

During my twenty years of teaching, I have seen countless student writers who turned out polished, craftwise, screenplays but could not offer either a story or characters worth a moment's interest. It was during those years that I learned craft is relatively easy—most of it can be taught in a few hours—but artistry is a gift and cannot be taught in a few years, if at all.

It is little wonder that after all these years, Dan O'Bannon, who has artistry flowing out of his pores, concentrates on craft when he writes his screenplays. When I asked him what is the true formula for success in a screenplay, Dan replied, "Three acts and a conflict."

If you've got the artistry to know in your guts what is a powerful story and what are compelling characters, then you can think about conventional structure. But, without great gut instinct, following formulas is a waste of time.

To show you how differently each screenwriter writes, let me turn to Joe Eszterhas (*Basic Instinct, F.I.S.T., Flashdance, Jagged Edge, Music Box,* and others). Joe is, at the time I write this, the highest-paid screenwriter in the history of the movies. *Basic Instinct* alone was sold for *three million dollars,* and he sold a second script in the same year, *Original Sin,* for *one million five hundred and fifty thousand dollars.* (To date, *Basic Instinct* has grossed over 100 million dollars. The screenplay was a bargain.)

So surely the man with the "formula" for success is Joe Eszterhas.

I asked Joe if he worked in a three-act structure and he replied:

"No, I just start writing. And sometimes I don't know where it's going to go. That's when it gets really exciting to me, when I don't know where it's going to go, because it's not locked in, it's not set."

Ask yourself: Is there a formula? And I'll give you the answer: Write what you truly believe in, what excites you, what you care about—the kind of movie that *you* would pay money to see. *That's the formula.* It's buried inside of every screenwriter who ever sat down to write a screenplay and even those who write standing up and even those who write their screenplays while sitting in the bathtub, like Dalton Trumbo (*Spartacus, Johnny Got His Gun,* etc.), one of the greatest screenwriters who ever lived.

You are the formula; use it, exercise it, develop it—nobody else in this world has one like it.

In the final analysis, you, alone, must decide if your screenplay works or does not work. Listen to constructive criticism and accept any informed opinions or ideas that you feel are worthwhile, but avoid like the plague any that you feel aren't worthwhile.

Summing Up

To create a good middle to your screenplay is no mystery. Just ask yourself what are the *obstacles*, what are the *problems*, your protagonist must overcome. Add new elements if needed. Overcoming obstacles is what will escalate the dramatic tension and the conflict you need to write drama.

"Put your hero up a tree and throw rocks at him." That is the essence of your middle.

No matter how many pages it takes, your middle should build to the *final confrontation*, head on, between the protagonist(s) and the antagonist(s). This is the ultimate clash of opposing forces. This is the climax of your movie, no matter who wins or who loses.

The End

We have said that a theme is a proposition leading to a conclusion. The last section of your movie, and the shortest, is your conclusion. It is where the theme is most often stated, either explicitly or implicitly, if you have not done so sooner. It is where the audience (reader) learns the meaning of the movie, what it was *saying*.

Plenty of movies get by without saying anything.

Outstanding examples of movies that say nothing are *Batman* and *Batman Returns*. The themes of these movies appear to be that if you spend enough money on promotion, you can sell megamillions of dollars worth of merchandise. When interviewed about *Batman* in *Details* magazine, director Tim Burton said, "There were parts I liked, but overall it was boring." It's a comment that I think could apply to both movies. But the first one is reportedly the highest-grossing box-office champ of all time. Go figure.

Your writing will go much easier and your script will be so much more satisfying to you if you *do* have something to say in your story. Why settle for the second-rate when, with less effort, you can go first-class?

The end is the resolution of the story as well as the conclusion of the theme. *It is that which nothing need follow.* It should be a *catharsis*, a relieving of emotional tensions.

Of course, audiences like happy endings—everybody does—in life as well as in drama. However, contrary to Hollywood's obsession with happy endings as a way to box-office success, some of our greatest films have won critical acclaim, Oscars, and big box-office with unhappy endings. Here are some examples:

The Bridge on the River Kwai is a film that superbly stands the test of time. Written by blacklisted writers Michael Wilson and Carl Foreman but credited to Pierre Boulle, author of the novel on which it is based, it ends with the protagonist killed, the bridge destroyed, and the young doctor shouting to the camera, "It's madness! Madness!" This is a very satisfying and successful anti-war movie. That the major characters are all killed and their whole enterprise comes to naught did not in any way hinder the success of this movie.

Cabaret, the brilliantly filmed musical based on Christopher Isherwood's *Berlin Stories*, ends with a pull-back shot of the nightclub as seen through a beveled glass door. We see the club packed with customers, many of whom are now wearing Nazi armbands, foreshadowing the coming of Hitler and the devastation he would bring with him. This film, winner of several Oscars, is a superb rendering of material that began life as short stories, then arrived on Broadway as a play, then, later, as a musical, and, finally, made its way to the screen. Screenwriters would do well to study this film of Jay Presson Allen's Academy Award-nominated screenplay. Ms. Allen shows us how to say a great deal with very few words. Her scene and story structure in this film is as good as it gets. Check out this movie and see a rare and superb example of musical-*drama*. (Director and choreographer Bob Fosse's genius has never been more abundantly displayed.) The dark theme of this film is that if we pretend life is a cabaret while outside the world is collapsing around us, we will lose everything we hold dear.

The Player, the much acclaimed dissection of Hollywood directed by Bob Altman, ends with the protagonist being blackmailed by a writer who knows he has gotten away with murder. Note that the "hero" of this movie is unlikable and unscrupulous, but *fascinating* in his machinations.

Patton is another classic with a downer ending. Like all the movies mentioned above, the protagonist is anything but "likable" but he is fascinating, so it matters not one whit whether he wins or loses; we are not "rooting for him."

More unhappy endings: William Goldman's excellent *A Bridge Too Far* and *Butch Cassidy and the Sundance Kid. Lawrence of Arabia* by master screenwriter Robert Bolt. *Sunset Boulevard, Ace in the Hole, Double Indemnity, The Postman Always Rings Twice, The Treasure of the Sierra Madre,* and on and on. The list of unhappy endings numbers in the hundreds. It's amazing how many classics come to us without conventional Hollywood happy endings or "likable" or even "rooting interest" protagonists. It's a wonder how little Hollywood studio executives have learned from this wealth of great American movies.

Happy endings are not necessary *provided* they contain a catharsis, a sense of relief, of "Yes, I understand. I know what this movie was about and it is a *believable* and acceptable ending." This is an *attitude* and an *understanding* you want to win from your audience.

The last thing in the world that you want from your audience is a "What was that all about?" reaction, which is a corollary to the even worse question "Why did I waste my time watching this movie?"

When you start your screenplay, you *must know* the attitudinal ending you want from your audience *before you begin.*

You do not have to know where and how the ending will take place—these things can come to you as you go along—but *you must know* what you want your audience *to feel* when the movie is over.

Here is an example of what I mean:

Some years back, there was a splendid, intimate movie called *Five Easy Pieces.* It was one of Jack Nicholson's earliest starring vehicles, and was superbly written by Adrien Joyce (Carole Eastman's pseudonym). It deservedly received an Academy Award nomination for Best Picture of the Year and garnered many rave reviews as well. This is the story of a loner (Nicholson) who suffers pain and guilt because of his alienation from his family, particularly his father. The line of action is a man desperate to escape his angst and find acceptance and peace, hopefully through some sort of catharsis, with his stern, aged, and infirm musician father.

The end of the film, as Ms. Joyce wrote it, is that Bobby Dupee (Nicholson) is unable to resolve his differences with his father or his family and is doomed to continue his life as an unhappy drifter.

The director, Bob Rafelson, told me that the night before they were to shoot the final scene of the film, he, Nicholson, and Ms. Joyce were hunkered down in a motel room on location arguing about what the ending of the movie should be. These were animated, sometimes heated, discussions. The question was, Does Bobby hit the road again, a drifting loner going nowhere or does he stay at home still fighting a losing battle against his father's emotional iron curtain?

Finally, in the wee hours of the morning, it was decided that Bobby would be last seen out on the highway, alone, bumming a ride to anywhere.

Rafelson told me that they all realized it didn't matter whether Bobby stayed home or hit the road. The *details* or even the *action* of the ending was unimportant. What counted was that, *in either case*, the *attitudinal ending* was true to the writer's vision of the story: Bobby Dupee was and would remain a lost soul, still unable to resolve his issues with his father and family. Whether he remained at home or hit the road made no difference. Ms. Joyce's theme was validated in either case.

If you know your theme, the conclusion to your proposition, then the details of how you validate it can come to you as you write.

Jake the Explainer

In all too many mysteries, the end consists of the police and or a private eye confronting a room full of suspects and explaining who committed the crime, how it was done, and why. This dreadful cliché, sometimes called "Jake the explainer," is, alas, the easy way out for lazy writers. Jake is the character (by whatever name) whose job it is to tell the audience the who, what, when, or how of the crime. Perhaps "Jake" is sometimes (rarely) unavoidable. Do your best to look for a better way out. The best solution to this problem is to feed out the information on the crime, and whodunit, a little at a time in the last section of your screenplay.

Blake Edwards and William Peter Blatty gave us an hilarious send-up of "Jake the Explainer" in the outstanding comedy *A Shot in the Dark*. The final scene has Inspector Clouseau (Peter Sellers) confront all the suspects in a perfect parody of inept movie mysteries. It's classic comedy.

Deus Ex Machina

This dreadful device, "the machine of God," is something no worthwhile writer should ever fall prey to. This consists of writing a sudden, out-of-nowhere (from the heavens), easy solution to your plot. It should be avoided at all costs.

The Three Penny Opera, the brilliant opera by Bertolt Brecht and Kurt Weill, ends with a rousing musical number parodying the deus ex machina device. A rider on a white horse gallops down the theatre aisles and onto the stage bearing a messenger who announces that Queen Victoria has pardoned Mack the Knife and all criminals throughout the land!

Gilbert and Sullivan also parodied the deus ex machina device in *Pirates of Penzance* with a comic musical number telling us that all the pirates are now free, pardoned by the queen.

In movies, sometimes the deus ex machina is more subtly but just as obnoxiously displayed. In *Patriot Games*, an otherwise well-crafted melodrama, the climax happens when our hero (Harrison Ford) leaps into a small boat on a black and stormy night and goes roaring off into the Atlantic in pursuit of the villain. In a clumsy confrontation, our hero happens upon the one boat on this dark and stormy sea that contains the villain who, as it happens, has killed off his aides so that when Jack Ryan (Ford) finally pulls alongside, they can have a rousing mano-a-mano battle to guess-whose death. No matter how disguised it is by action piled upon action, it is still deus ex machina, and it becomes laughable as a consequence.

Leave the deus ex machina to Gilbert and Sullivan and other masters of musical comedy.

Good Endings

Find a good ending that is (1) honest to your characters, theme, and story; (2) satisfying; and (3) not boring.

Casablanca — As Claude Rains and Humphrey Bogart stroll off into the airport fog and Bogart says, "Louis, this could be the start of a beautiful friendship." It confirms the theme: We can not remain cynically neutral, above the battle, against tyranny; we must commit ourselves to the forces of freedom. *We are all in this battle together.*

Great endings often say it all visually, with few, if any, words needed. The members of the audience seem to be particularly gratified if they can *see* the meaning of the story without being told what it is.

Driving Miss Daisy — The last scene, as the chauffeur feeds Miss Daisy in the nursing home, is a bit sentimental but the perfect visual conclusion of a universal theme: Yes, we are our brothers' keeper, and we all need a friend.

Class Action — Gene Hackman dances with his daughter, a symbolic resolution of their long-time animosity. It resolves the theme: Family love and mutual support counts more than being a winning lawyer.

Talking About It

I cannot over-stress the importance of dialogue in your screenplay; it is your ticket to success or oblivion in Hollywood.

Great dialogue is immediately recognizable because the reader can *immediately* recognize if the screenwriter is putting words in the mouths of the characters or the characters are speaking for themselves. This is not a debatable point.

You *must know* your characters well enough *for them to speak for themselves.* As pointed out earlier, this does not mean you need to develop a full biography of your characters, you only need to know enough to see and hear them in your mind's eye. Nothing more, but nothing less.

It is a sad fact of movie life that most people who read screenplays professionally read only the dialogue. It's quick, it's in the center of the page, it's easy. These professional readers know that if the dialogue crackles, if it's exciting, the rest of the script is apt to be worth reading as well.

Here is a bizarre, true story that illustrates how professional readers read screenplays.

Back in 1958, I was under contract to Columbia Pictures

Television (then known as Screen Gems) as a writer-producer and was assigned to produce two 90-minute movies for CBS-TV's outstanding live drama series, "Playhouse 90." Understandably, CBS simply could not turn out a top level of live 90-minute drama every week. We were to provide them with a few 90-minute mini-movies to help take the pressure off the live production staff.

The mini-movie I was working on, *Before I Die*, was on the lot shooting when I got a call from the Assistant Director telling me I was needed on stage at once.

I rushed to the lot where I found the crew standing around muttering to themselves; they were stalled over something, unable to shoot.

It turned out that the director had sent for me because he was having difficulty understanding the scene he was supposed to be shooting.

He took me aside for a hurried sotto voce conference. He pointed to the offending scene in his script.

"It makes no sense," he said.

I studied it for a few minutes and saw no problem whatsoever. (I had spent six weeks working on the script myself, preparing it for production.) I quickly pointed to the descriptive heading of the scene in question.

"It's all here," I told the director, "in the scene set-up, perfectly described." It was a particularly long scene set-up, perhaps 1/4 of a page.

The director read the section to which I was pointing. His face turned beet red.

"My God," he said, "of course the scene makes sense, but, although I'm ashamed to admit it, I never read the introduction to it."

I returned to my office; the director completed our 90-minute movie, did a splendid job, and *Before I Die* was nominated by the Screen Producers Guild for Best Produced Television Motion Picture of 1958.

This incident at the very beginning of my TV movie career taught me a valuable lesson: Readers, even some directors, *read only the dialogue* in the screenplay. They merely scan all descriptive or narrative material.

If you want to be a winning player in this tough game called Hollywood screenwriting, make certain your dialogue comes to life on the printed page. Dialogue does not have to be witty or funny, but it helps enormously.

Real Dialogue Versus Movie Dialogue

The way people actually talk to each other and movie dialogue have nothing in common. Your job as a dramatist is to create the *illusion* of real dialogue. It is easy only if you work very hard at it, edit yourself carefully, rewrite it endlessly, polish it, until the characters say only *what must be said and nothing else.*

My best advice for writing dialogue is cut, then cut some more, and when you think you've got it right, cut still more. Make it, as we say, lean and mean.

What you're writing will *seem* like conversation if your characters talk like only these particular characters would. Which is to say, like themselves.

One way to judge the viability of your dialogue is to read it aloud, all the parts, often. Play the scene, play it into a tape recorder, then listen back to it. Is it wordy, boring, unreal, ambling, off the point? In actual conversation, people ramble on; they are repetitive, redundant, meandering, unresponsive, often boring. In short, we all too often talk just for the sake of talking.

This simple dialogue test will work for you: Cover the characters' names on the page, then read the dialogue. If you can't tell one character's lines from another, you are off the mark. You should be able to distinguish between each of the characters just by reading their dialogue. No two people (or characters) talk alike. Check it out.

Avoid using bizarre spelling to suggest dialects. Only a dash of flavoring is needed to suggest different accents or languages.

Even as I implore you not to write in dialect, I am mindful of one of one of the most unusual student screenplays I have ever read.

It was written by Alex Cox, a young man from Liverpool, England. It was written *entirely* in Liverpudlian dialect *and* spelling. It was both outrageous and one of the best student screenplays I have ever read, even though I could not translate some of the words!

Alex was a delightful young student with a great and wicked sense of humor. All of us at UCLA loved him and are delighted, but not surprised, by his success. May his career blossom further. My comments about not writing in dialect remind me of a funny and familiar axiom: *Beware of all generalities, including this one.*

Movie dialogue is *carefully structured,* polished to a high gloss, witty, succinct, and to the point. And when it's good, it seems more real than the real thing.

At least part of the reason for this is that audiences want to believe it's real. When they enter the movie theatre or turn on their TV, they have made a decision to suspend disbelief and, once they begin to like the movie, they want to believe the characters are really talking like people talk. This is why some members of the audience think the actors are making up the dialogue as they go along. And this is one reason why the screenwriter is often denigrated. The more real the writer can make the characters appear to be, the more invisible he or she becomes.

Pinter Versus Chayefsky

There are, basically, two opposing schools of movie dialogue writing, each the opposite end of the screenwriting spectrum: the noted British playwright and screenwriter Harold Pinter and the equally brilliant and supremely talented Paddy Chayefsky.

Pinter is a famous minimalist, for whom long and weighty pauses often say what words cannot. He is a very effective dramatist. I suggest that you see Pinter's excellent movie *The Turtle Diary* to get a first-hand understanding of how well minimal dialogue can work for you. Pinter's work illustrates a truism about movie dialogue: The most important lines are often the ones not spoken.

At the other end of the dialogue spectrum is the late, great Paddy Chayefsky (*Marty, The Middle of the Night, The Americanization of Emily, The Hospital, Network*, and others) who fervently believed that his words were as important to his movies as were the pictures. And he proved it in movie after movie.

Many critics agree that Chayefsky's "ear for dialogue" has no peer in screenwriting history. Chayefsky achieved a naturalness that was uncanny in making you believe that you were hearing the hearts and souls of his characters speaking out.

Here is what Chayefsky had to say in his interview with John Brady about how he wrote his dialogue: "I write laboriously worked-out dialogue . . . because I know what I want my characters to say. I envision the scene; I can imagine them up there on the screen; I try to imagine what they would be saying and how they would be saying it, and I keep it in character. And the dialogue comes out of that. I think that goes for every writer in the world. Then I rewrite it. Then I cut it. Then I refine it until I get the scene as precisely as I can get it." [John Brady,

Craft of the Screenwriter, Simon & Schuster, 1981.]

What all this spells out is work, work, and more work. As Chayefsky is saying, dialogue is the art of editing, structuring, polishing, refining, and making it as perfect as humanly possible. Don't settle for less. Check out some of Chayefsky's movies and hear dialogue as you have never heard it before. Here is a story about the uniqueness of Chayefsky's dialogue, and the reverence that the industry has for it.

When the screenplay for *The Hospital* was first submitted to United Artists, the studio executives all agreed that it was brilliant and they wanted to film it. "But, what were we going to do with all that dialogue?" a studio executive told me at the time, "speeches a full page long, and some even longer! It was the wordiest screenplay any of us had ever read. But we had an even bigger problem. Rod Steiger was attached to the screenplay; he had an option on it, and we knew that all those torrents of words in Steiger's mouth would put the audience sound asleep. We decided to wait until Steiger's option ran out and then offer it to the only actor who could carry page-long speeches and hold an audience's attention: George C. Scott."

According to plan, U.A. didn't move on the script until Steiger was out of the picture, then they got a go-ahead from George C. Scott, and, soon after, *The Hospital* went into production. Unfortunately, *The Hospital* didn't quite come together because, as Chayefsky later told John Brady, it had too many things going on, too many genres.

Network, however, works to perfection and is a must-see movie for every screenwriter, not only because of its brilliant dialogue but because of its ability to cut into the underbelly of network television and let everyone see why it is what it is. *Network* shows a master screenwriter at the peak of both his craft and his art.

It is essential to your success as a screenwriter that you let your characters speak to you and then, when they've finished, you edit the hell out of them. No amount of time you spend on polishing your dialogue is wasted. Just remember: *Dialogue is what gets read.*

Readability

Here are some important tips on how to make your screenplay reader-friendly.

Keep all descriptive material to an absolute minimum. Do not describe the furniture, the decor, *unless its character is exceptional and important to your story*. You only need to give a *sense* of what the location is like. My favorite example of maximum economy and originality is described in Sterling Silliphant's interview in *The Screenwriter Looks at the Screenwriter* when we discussed keeping the screenplay lean, eliminating clutter and unnecessary material. (Sterling won an Academy Award for *In the Heat of the Night* and is one of the most prolific—and one of the best—writers of motion-pictures and television. His industry recognition came in the form of his established fee, one million dollars per screenplay.) Listen to Sterling, he is a wise man:

"I have progressed to the point now where I have learned to write a shorthand script which, somehow, maybe because of my specific choice of words, which are emotion-laden words, will in the very sparse and brief stage directions create a mood, so in a sense it's a shorthand poem. Stage directions are very brief. I usually have no adjectives, no adverbs, frequently not even verbs. For instance, in *The New Centurions*, it says INTERIOR APARTMENT - Shitty. That's all. One word. Then the dialogue starts. That's what I mean.

"I have learned not to put under the character who is about to say some dialogue a stage direction, such as 'softly' or 'with great feeling' or 'crying out.' I drop all that."

I asked Sterling, "You feel the line speaks for itself?"

Sterling replied, "If it doesn't, you'd better rewrite it."

Let me stress this point about directing the actors a bit more. Take the line

                         JOHN
                       (shouts)
                      Get out!

I urge you to eliminate the direction "(shouts)." In the first place, you are the writer, not the actor or the director. In the second place, the actor may whisper the words "Get out" and get more force and power out of the line than your direction to shout. Finally, by telling the actor how to act and the director how to direct, you are angering both of them and stamping yourself an amateur in the process. Like it or not, you have to trust your collaborators.

After over twenty years of reading student screenplays, my personal bugaboo is the writer who feels he or she must direct—not only the actor's line readings but the actor's physical movements. Case in point: the rank amateur will always reveal himself or herself with this dreadful direction to the actors: "he turns," "she turns." Why does the novice feel it is necessary to tell the actors how to move? Do they imagine that these talented folks are helpless to perform without directions from the writer? Do they think the director is asleep on the job? None of these are the case. Yet hapless and insecure writers still find it incumbent upon themselves to not only write the script but to direct the actors and direct the director. In a word: *don't.* The only loser in this naive, ignorant, and egocentric style of screenwriting is the writer. The lesson of writing the screenplay is: *less is more.*

After Completing the Screenplay

After you've finished the screenplay and put it away for a couple of days, do your best not to even think about it. When you feel you can come back to it fresh, bring it out and read it start to finish at one sitting. Then, and only then, begin your rewriting. It will come as no news to you that all writing is rewriting. Often, the next time through it will give you insights and ideas for revisions that will improve the screenplay at least fifty percent. You will be quite surprised at how much better it will get on this first major rewrite after completion of the first draft.

Rewrite and rewrite until you are certain that the screenplay is as good as you can make it. Then, and only then, have it *professionally typed, error-free,* and show a few copies to friends whose opinions you trust. Have about ten copies made, no more. You don't want copies of your script circulating all over the place like yesterday's newspaper. Remember, it is, indeed, a "property." You wouldn't loan your car to twenty or thirty friends to see how they like it. Treat your work with the respect it deserves.

Never submit a screenplay or any sample of your writing to *anyone in the professional world of filmmaking until it is as good as you can possibly make it.* You've only got one shot with this script, and you've put too many hours and too much hard work into it to blow it at this final stage.

Never make a professional submission with a comment or even a hint that you have further changes in mind and are only waiting for more feedback before doing them. Once you hand your *completed, polished final draft* to the world of Hollywood, you are officially on stage, the curtain has gone up—this is your professional debut. You are *in the marketplace.* You are a screenwriter now, and you can fully and proudly acknowledge it. Never sell yourself short on this point. Be proud of your accomplishment, it's no mean feat; you deserve to pat yourself on the back.

Now settle back and savor that great moment of completion and catharsis . . . and start to think about the next movie you'd like to write.

Selling
the
Script

How to Get an Agent

The continuous infusion of new talent is the lifeblood of entertainment industry agents. They cannot survive without being on the lookout for new writers, actors, producers, directors, etc. The bigger agencies even have young men and women (junior agents) on staff whose primary purpose is to come up with and represent new and talented people.

This does not mean, however, that the agent's door will be opened for you by eager young agents with open arms. *You must open the door yourself.*

For writers it is not all that difficult if you have at least one "show" script or calling-card screenplay that demonstrates your ability as a screenwriter of exceptional talent. I suggest that you have two or more show scripts, each one polished to as close to perfection as you can make it. These screenplays are your passport into a future career in the entertainment industry. There is *no better method of entry.*

The question that you will always be asked is, "What have you written?" which will be followed quickly by, "May I read it?"

If you are thinking about becoming a screenwriter but have no completed, polished screenplays as solid evidence that you are serious, forget it. The world is full of wannabe screenwriters who talk about the script they are presently writing or plan to write. This is not a commitment to becoming a screenwriter; this is a poor commitment to *wanting to become a writer* and it is worth less than the air in your tires. If you want to build a career as a screenwriter, start now by writing screenplays. Nobody in Hollywood has any interest whatsoever in writers who talk a great game but can't deliver the screenplay.

Let's assume you do have some screenplays you feel are ready to show. What then?

Networking is a great key to getting started in Hollywood. And, most likely, you will have to *be in Hollywood* to launch your career. That's where the action is, no doubt about it.

Go through your memory bank and see if you can recall anybody you know, even casually, who knows somebody who knows somebody who works in the movie industry.

If you don't know anyone who knows anyone who can, through any kind of contact, get your script to an agent, then do the next best thing. The Writers Guild of America, west, regularly publishes in its *Journal* an up-to-date list of all writers' agents in Hollywood, with asterisks beside the names of those who will read unsolicited manuscripts. Send one dollar and a self-addressed, stamped envelope to WGA, west at 8955 Beverly Blvd., Los Angeles, CA 90048 and request the most current list.

Go over this list and select the agent you would like to contact, based on whatever fragment of information you have heard about them, or merely based on your gut instinct.

Almost all agents are legitimate business people, there to provide a service and make a living for themselves in the process. Stories about wicked, conniving agents are generally pure fiction. But agents are tough-minded citizens in a tough-minded business. They have little time for nonsense. It is possible to build a career without an agent, but highly inadvisable. Agents earn their ten percent, no doubt about it.

Never, under any circumstances, pay anybody anything to read your screenplay. So-called "agents" who advertise that they will read your screenplay for a fee are to be *avoided at all costs.* They are not worth the postage it costs to mail the script and are marginal characters at best. Some writers I know never even got their screenplays back from these phony "agents" who, nonetheless, kept the writers' money.

Stick to the normal, routine, time-tested methods for finding an agent. It has worked for generations and continues to work remarkably well.

When you have chosen, by whatever method, an agent to whom you would like to submit your material, write him or her a letter requesting them to read your screenplay. Do not send the screenplay until you get a reply. It is probably a good idea to write several agents at the same time and to send your script to the one who responds first or whose response pleases you most.

Do not spend money on a fancy cover for your screenplay. It is meaningless; what counts is what's inside. A good title is a plus. Spend some time thinking about the title and make sure you are totally happy with it. *Do not suggest alternate titles.* You don't want to present yourself as that insecure even before they read your script.

Make certain your letter is well-written and to the point. *Do not include a synopsis of your screenplay or divulge its contents.* It is enough to say you have a screenplay that you believe is saleable in the current movie marketplace. Make sure your letter reflects the work of an intelligent, mature, sincere writer of exceptional talent. You will initially be judged by this introductory letter. If you write a great letter, they'll read your script. If you don't, they won't.

You may not get a response for some weeks. If a month passes, write to still another agent or, if your patience is running out, phone the office of the agent to whom you wrote and speak to his or her secretary. *Politely inquire* if they received your letter. Keep in mind that an agent's secretary may very well become your friend in court if she or he likes dealing with you on the phone. It is always a good idea to try to strike up some sort of cordial relationship with any and all secretaries in offices where you might be doing business. Secretaries control the ebb and flow of the offices in which they work. It is in their power to help ease one screenplay to the attention of the agent over other screenplays.

Eventually you will get a response from the agents to whom you write, and in some cases, but not all, you will be invited to send your screenplay. Do so promptly and with a polite and agreeable cover letter, stating the particular attributes you feel this screenplay has for the marketplace and *major casting ideas you have or major directors you think would be right for this project.* (Again, *do not include a synopsis of your screenplay or story.* It will only undercut the surprise of discovery the agent will get in reading it. A synopsis is not likely to help you sell an idea. Only a reading of your full screenplay will do that.)

Now you come to the time when your greatest patience is required. It will seem like an eternity before the agent gets back to you.

But you are not helpless. There are several things you can do to help your cause. After a month or so, you can phone the agent's secretary and *politely* inquire whether or not the office received your screenplay and politely ask if he or she has any idea how long it might take before the agent gets back to you. If you become hostile or bitter, you will only harm yourself.

The key in this conversation is that you must treat the secretary as a potential ally, not as the enemy. Any anger on your part, or even impoliteness, will be self-destructive. Every agent's office is flooded with screenplays at all times. Yours is a singular case only to you. To everybody else, it is just another screenplay somewhere in the to-be-read pile. Your ability to be *agreeably aggressive* at this stage is crucial.

If, after more weeks than you can bear, you feel the need to press on and get some action going, then by all means *send your screenplay with another cover letter to another agent.* You are under no obligation to the first agent when they do not respond. If necessary (and I doubt it will be), send your screenplay and cover letter to still a third agent, and even a fourth. It's your career, not theirs.

But do not flood the market with copies of your screenplay. You do not want every agent in town (Hollywood is a very small town) to mention your script. If it is too readily available, it will lose some of its value. I suggest that you never have more than five or six copies out in the marketplace, or with agents, at the same time. You must avoid local citizens saying to one another, "Oh, yes, I've already read that." It becomes yesterday's news.

You could find yourself in for anywhere from a two to four month wait for any responses. Wait no longer. Starting your career as a screenwriter is not for the faint of heart.

Suppose you eventually hear from a couple of agents and each of them wants to represent your screenplay? *Use the telephone.* Talk to each of the agents who expresses interest and choose the one with whom you have the best rapport and in whom you feel confidence based on his or her approach to selling your screenplay.

Remember, agents are not in business to hear themselves soft-talk clients. They have to get out there and meet their overhead, which is only possible when they sell the work of the people they represent. They have no time to waste on writers they don't believe they can sell. If they respond favorably to your material, they are serious, they are determined to sell it; short of that, you would never hear from them, I assure you.

What kind of agency should you choose, little one, big one, famous, not-so-famous? They come in all sizes and each size offers advantages and disadvantages. It's a trial-and-error decision. Choose one based on your gut instinct (after all, that's what you used to write the screenplay) and see how it works out. If you have a real rapport with the agent who likes your screenplay and who lays out a sales plan that seems right to you, then go with that one. There are no guarantees, not in the entertainment industry, no matter how rich and famous you become.

Briefly, here are the key differences between going with a big, powerful talent agency and going with a smaller office.

In the big agencies, you get the advantage of having immediate access to their entire list of powerful clients—big-name stars, directors, and producers. This is a very real advantage. On the other hand, as a new writer, you will be shunted aside, in the beginning, to a junior agent whose chief attribute is that he can forward you along the command chain to the big, important agents in his office. The junior agent, in these situations, often functions as a referral service, but a *valuable* referral service. If you like the junior agent you are assigned to, you may very well develop a lifelong friendship and business relationship. There is no doubt that the power of the entertainment industry rests in the hands of a very few men, and they are the superagents of Hollywood.

On the other hand, if you sign with a small office, you will get more personal attention and even some T.L.C. if your agent feels your talent warrants it. The small agency will get more excited by finding a hot, new screenwriter than will the big agency. But the small agencies, in turn, often have to work through the mega-agents to get access to the big-name actors and directors.

The writer-agent relationship is the definition of symbiosis: two different kinds of organisms thrown together for mutual advantage and mutual interdependence. The lament of almost every writer, actor, et al. in town is how difficult it is to get their agent on the phone. It's absolutely true. It *is* difficult. Patience, persistence, and passion are the operative words here as well. After you become rich and famous, you will never need to worry about getting your agent on the phone (until you are among the *were* rich-and-famous).

It is a fact of Hollywood life that agents are likely to be driving Mercedes while their clients are driving Toyotas. The reason is simple: Agents "handle" scores of clients; a few of their clients are kept working, making megabucks, and their commissions carry the rest of the less fortunate. The agent with a good client list is always far ahead of the game. It's like being the house in Las Vegas.

Still, like them or not, they are a necessary element in Hollywood's movie-TV game.

Let's take the best-case scenario: You make a sale.

Once you have a contract to sell movie or television material or go to work as a movie or TV writer, you may join the Writers Guild of America, west. Or, if you live in the New York area, you may choose to join WGA, east. The two organizations are affiliated but not the same. All too often there is rivalry between them.

You may not join WGA until you have sold material or are under contract as a movie or TV writer. The benefits of joining WGA are so rich and worthwhile that no writer in his or her right mind would refuse.

Though the WGA is an open union, open to everybody who has sold material, joining it is both a must and a privilege. The benefits of being a member of this best of all unions are so many and so widely ranging that the Guild offers a booklet describing them.

There probably isn't a screenwriter alive who, at one point or another in his or her career, hasn't had some sort of beef with the guild. (Put any two writers together and you have twenty-nine opinions about the Guild.) Yet I can't imagine anyone who doesn't get down on his or her knees and thank God for this super organization that protects us from the predators who swim in the Hollywood seas, hoping to feed off writers. The reality is that we are the only natural resource in the movie or TV industry (with the exception of actors) without whom the studios would eventually have to shut down their factories. The WGA is there to protect us from the sharks and, worse, ourselves. (The WGA is the only Hollywood union that manages to sabotage itself in every strike.)

How to Keep Your Agent Working for You

Agents are just like everybody else—a new client, like a new car or a new home, is exciting and will tend to get an extraordinary amount of care and attention. However, when the newness wears off, the client, not unlike the new car and the new home, tends to be taken for granted *unless the new client shows outstanding talent early in the relationship.*

Keeping your agent working for you with enthusiasm is not easy. *You must keep working for yourself.* After a flurry of success, the initial honeymoon period passes and you may find that it is difficult to get your agent on the phone. It is not because he or she wants to ignore you, it is just that new and more exciting people have arrived on the scene and the agent has *at least* a score of other clients who also need attention. Do not despair; this is awful, but it is also commonplace.

In Hollywood, you come to understand early on that networking is the key to success. Everybody knows everybody else and the key word in town is "relationships."

If you've ever met or had a phone conversation with somebody in the entertainment industry, it is then said that you have a "relationship" with that person.

Once screenwriters have established themselves, they do not need relationships to the degree that people in the other creative areas do. The screenplay still speaks for itself. But, in the beginning, networking and relationships are the key ingredients to success. Everybody in this most uncertain and insecure field of endeavor wants to work with people they know.

The many friendships made in film school often carry over to long-term working relationships in Hollywood. This is but one reason why film school is valuable to beginning screenwriters. The friends you make there may be friends for a lifetime.

It is not commonplace for writers to remain with the same agent for their entire careers and yet a few of them do. This involves a lot of give and take, a lot of flexibility on both sides. Often, agents are as good as you demand they be. I highly recommend you remain with the same agent as long as possible, knowing full well that you have to be as productive as you expect him or her to be. Once either one of you sits back to rest on your laurels, the relationship will be non-productive and of no use to either one of you.

I had many agents during my forty-year tenure as a writer-producer in Hollywood. I seemed to change agents about once every five years, not by pre-ordained plan, only because that's the way it seemed to work out. Fortunately, I have remained friends with all of the agents who represented me over my long career. I came to like and respect agents. I am happily married to a former screenwriters' agent.

If ever in your career you feel a need to change agents, *talk to him or her about it first.* The chances are, if you're unhappy, he or she is unhappy and you will part friends or, at least, improve your working relationship.

When an agent initially approaches you, he or she will want you to sign a three-year contract. Try to make it for one or two years, but in the end, sign it. The Writers Guild contract with the Association of Talent Agencies guarantees members that they are free to leave an agent if the agent has not gotten them a writing job in ninety days. In any event, few agents will force you to remain with them if you want to leave.

Get accustomed to the idea that you must generate a lot of your work yourself through your own contacts. The bottom line is that you are and always will be the best seller of yourself and your talent.

Don't be shy about it. Hollywood was not invented for or by shy people. In a remarkably brief period of time, you will lose all vestiges of shyness if you are to thrive and survive.

TV or Not TV

Once considered the ghetto of Hollywood, the enormous incomes and employment opportunities television now presents to writers, producers, directors, actors, agents, et al. have made the medium a popular and sought-after marketplace. Though it is still ranked an inferior and somewhat unwelcome relative to feature-film work, it, nonetheless, can no longer be ignored by aspiring screenwriters. Sure, everybody in Hollywood wants to work in features, but nobody is immune to making big bucks, even if their social status is somewhat tarnished.

Television, itself, has status rungs on its ladder of employment. If you write mini-series or movies-for-TV, you are assumed to be a superior writer to those who write episodic TV. However, comedy writers who limit themselves to episodic TV work are considered somewhat lower on the Hollywood talent scale.

The reality is that if you write the world's best episode of "Harry Hunk, Gladiator" or "Sex Kittens on Mars," you will still be considered a writer only capable of writing TV series episodes. In spite of the substantial money now available to episodic TV writers (with residuals and syndication sales, a TV freelancer can finally earn as much as $50,000 for writing a single episode of "Northern Exposure"!), you will do yourself a lot more good and enhance your future career to a far greater degree if you spend almost the same amount of time writing a feature-length screenplay on speculation. Writers Guild rules wisely forbid a writer to write on spec or demand for a producer, agent, or any prospective employer. But everybody, including the Guild, applauds the writer who daringly risks a lot of time and hard work to introduce themselves as a screenwriter with an original screenplay.

Even if you should opt for episodic TV, there is no assurance that eager employers are awaiting you. There are very few assignments actually available (most TV series are staff-written), and the few open assignments often go to well-established TV episode writers. In the long haul, you are probably much better off putting your efforts into writing screenplays. (Write and sell just one screenplay and, if it gets filmed, you will be forever after elevated to a higher status in Hollywood.)

Writing Episodic TV

If you are determined to write episodic TV, you can get all the information you want on any given show by phoning the offices of the series that you would like to write for (the name of the production company is always on the end of the on-screen credits). The format for each series is different, and so are the show's particular requirements. Do not attempt to write a TV series episode on spec *without first getting that show's requirements and format.*

Phone the production company and speak to the producer's secretary. Ask what the show's writing situation is, if they have any openings, and, most importantly, if they have a commitment for a long run. Most series have been cancelled or are about to be cancelled by the time you get around to calling.

It is true that some currently successful Hollywood

screenwriters did get their start in episodic TV, but they are few and far between. Writing for episodic TV is most certainly going about starting a screenwriting career the hard way.

Living Where the Work Is

To get started as a screenwriter and, especially, as a TV writer, you are going to have to live in or around Los Angeles. New York is a poor second choice.

A few writers have made it by mail, but they are the rare exceptions. Not a few screenwriters, *after* they've established themselves, move out of L.A. and commute for necessary meetings, etc.

This is not, however, true for television writers. They *must be* on hand, ready for fast revisions, quick meetings, sudden assignments, work to suit the fast-paced and im-possible-deadline world of television.

Hard Comedy

If you have the very rare gift of being able to write hard (big-laugh) comedy, launching your career writing television is a different matter altogether. Talented com-edy writers are *always in demand.* I make an important distinction between the hard-comedy writer and the soft (chuckles-and-grins) comedy writers. Soft-comedy writ-ers are a dime a dozen. Hard comedy writers would do well to develop their talent in television, where the incomes are astronomical and the recognition is strong and imme-diate. My former students who write hard comedy do not live an easy life but they bring their money home in skiploaders. ("Funny is money," a comedy-writing former student of mine recently told me.)

Cable Television

With the proliferation of made-for-television movies

by cable-television companies, an entirely new and significant marketplace has opened up for screenwriters. The money is nowhere near as significant as it is for theatrical-release movies but, often just as importantly, *your screenplay will get filmed.* When the major studios turned down Anna Hamilton Phelan's original screenplay *Into the Homeland* about militant white-supremacist groups in America, she took it to HBO, who filmed it with Anna as executive producer. HBO recently filmed a controversial screenplay about abortion, yet the networks refuse to touch the subject.

The more buyers there are, the more opportunities there are for screenwriters to explore controversial and important subject matter. It appears that movies-for-cable will become an ever-increasing marketplace for aspiring as well as established screenwriters.

TV Made Easier

If your heart and soul is in television series writing, here's a quick tip. Study the series you want to write until you know every running character—how they behave, their attitude, their mannerisms, etc. Learn what kind of stories the series does best and, most particularly, the strengths and weaknesses of the leading characters.

Stay away from unpopular series no matter how much you may like them. Unpopular series have a way of dropping off the schedule quickly. Stick with series of long-standing success and reputation. Before you write a line, write to the Writers Guild of America, west and ask them to send you a copy of their current "TV Market List." It is updated regularly, costs five dollars, and is definitely worth the money.

Odds and Ends

There are approximately 8,000 members of the Writers Guild of America, west. At any given time, the majority of them are out of work, unless they are wise enough to be using their time off to write spec screenplays on their own.

The Guild registers approximately 25,000 to 30,000 pieces of material every year (thousands of those are screenplays). There is a rumor that a skiploader arrives at the "Cheers" office once a month to haul away the unsolicited manuscripts sent to this megahit TV program.

If you obsess on any of these harsh realities of the marketplace before you begin to write, you are placing a crippling burden on yourself. Writers who focus on the odds for success are likely to strike out before they even pick up the bat.

The blunt and irrefutable truth is that new writers are *breaking into the Hollywood market every day of the week.* Nothing can stop them, unless they stop themselves. *The writers who make it big are never daunted by the odds.*

The odds are an abstraction and are completely meaningless. Your odds are as strong as your screenplay. And it makes no difference if you are female, old, black, yellow, green, or just escaped from prison. Your screenplay will eventually get read and judged by many people. If it is rejected, *it* is rejected, not you.

Always keep in mind that *it only takes one buyer to buy your screenplay.* This lesson was brought home to me many years ago by my agent at the time. I had written a screenplay that he much admired, but it had been turned down by all the major studios and some independents. Discouraged, I suggested to him that we put it in the files for the time being. "Nonsense," he said, "it's a good screenplay. We won't give up *because it only takes one person to like it.*" Within one month, he sold it, for what was at the time a sizable amount of money, to an important independent producer who loved it and hired me to produce it as well.

I have never forgotten my agent's important comment: "It only takes *one* person to like it." Don't you forget it.

The proper response to a lack of success with any given screenplay is ridiculously simple. Write another screenplay. Make it better and keep writing screenplays, developing and honing your art and craft until you discover for yourself that this is not the line of work for which you are best suited or that you have finally written yourself the key to your own success.

A sad but comforting consolation is that most of the unsolicited material arriving in Hollywood from wannabes are pretty dreadful. Talk to any reader, any professional in the business, and they will tell you about the poor quality of most of what they read. (My producer buddies regularly complain about it.) When a really good screenplay comes along, it's like striking a nugget while panning for gold. So, if you do write something outstanding, you may be assured that the odds will quickly change from seemingly impossible to highly likely, and you will get both an agent and recognition. Be of good cheer; the race has always gone to the swift but never to the faint of heart.

In Hollywood, your work is everything; personally, you are, alas, only a necessary "element" who comes with it. No, you won't be loved, not in Hollywood, not as a writer, no matter how brilliant your screenplays are. If you are looking for fame and fortune, Hollywood is your place. If you're looking for love or deeper appreciation, screenwriting is not your solution.

Who else in this world has so much control over their own destiny as the writer? They may denigrate you, curse you, even blacklist you (as they did so many screenwriters during the dark days of the McCarthy era), but they can not take away your talent or your ideas or your paper and pencil. (Several of those blacklisted screenwriters continued to write under different names and/or moved to England and reached great heights in their careers.)

You alone own your own mind. You are a member of the greatest profession in the world: *You are a writer.*

Digging Deeper

If you are to become a successful screenwriter, you are going to have to teach yourself to look at movies differently than you have ever looked at them before.

It is not helpful for you to see a movie superficially, to come away merely deciding if you enjoyed it or not. Instead, you are going to have to view and think about every movie you see *as a professional writer does*. You are going to have to look beneath the surface, to dig deep, to see what is *behind* the success or failure of a movie. You are going to have to *see the screenplay*.

Every time you see a movie, ask yourself the following questions.

(1) How do I know the genre?

(2) When do I know who the protagonist is, and how quickly is the *line of action* established?

(3) When is the *opposing force* identified? *Dramatic tension* probably begins *simultaneously*. How far into the film am I before this happens?

(4) What does the protagonist *need* and who or what stands in his or her way? This is much the same question as (3), but purposely rephrased for emphasis.

(5) What *characteristics* make the protagonist *worth watching*? Why am I *fascinated* by this character?

(6) How soon do I begin to sense the *theme* of the movie? How is it revealed to me?

(7) What is the core conflict of the story?

(8) What *surprises* are there? What scenes and story developments are unexpected? Which characters most fascinate me? Why do they fascinate me?

(9) Why does each scene work or not work? What is right or wrong with each scene? Which scenes are unnecessary? Look for the subtext of each scene and the words that are *not* spoken.

(10) What scenes are *implied* rather than shown? Make note of every story leap.

(11) What are the *complications* in the story? What makes the plot thicken?

(12) What is the *key element* of the movie that holds my *attention?*

(13) What in the movie is dramatically valid and what is not?

(14) How and why would I rewrite the movie?

Always see the screenplay. It is your best learning tool. And you will never stop learning.

As you begin to view movies in this way, you may have to see them more than once to get the knack of it. In time, however, *examining* and *studying* movies will become second nature to you. And it will become a lifelong habit.

Getting Going

Everybody has the capacity to be creative in one area of endeavor or another. Creativity is not the realm of only a select few.

Creativity is the result of freely exercising the "muscle" called imagination. Creativity is not easy. It is hard work that requires tough discipline.

Your first and most important step toward becoming a screenwriter must be a commitment to hard work—it is unavoidable if you are to succeed. During my many years of teaching screenwriting, I came to understand that those who were committed to hard work succeeded many times more often than those who had an abundance of talent, but were not committed to the job at hand.

Talent can't be taught, but creativity can be nourished and pushed to greater productivity and higher levels of achievement.

Following is a writing exercise that I used in my UCLA graduate screenwriting seminars. This exercise, which I call The Movie Game, helps to free the writer's imagination and develop a strong sense of what makes a good movie story.

The Movie Game™

The purpose of this game is to create and develop a full length movie story extemporaneously, making it up as you go along.

Although there are myriad variations to organizing this game, I find that playing it with a relatively small group of writers works best (I effectively use this game in my graduate seminars, which are limited to six students).

I like to start this game cold, at the beginning of a class session with no previous warning. That way, none of my writers has a chance to preconceive any ideas or stories and the game is kept purely spontaneous.

The rules are simple: one writer volunteers a scene, telling us *only what the audience would see on a movie screen*. Nothing can be told of what's in a character's mind *unless it is revealed through visible action on the screen or (only if necessary) told in dialogue (a poor second choice)*.

For example, a writer will suggest, "A young woman enters a phone booth and nervously makes a call; she is clearly upset."

"Where are we?" I ask him. *"What do we see on the screen?"*

"We are in a large mall in a big city; it is crowded," he replies, "and I haven't any idea who she's calling or what the call is about."

"Who knows why she's upset?" I ask the others.

"She just came from her doctor's office. He told her she is pregnant," a writer volunteers.

"She's calling her boyfriend," offers another writer, "and he tells her it's not his problem, he's not responsible."

Now our story is underway; we have dramatic tension and the potential for conflict—the most important elements of any drama.

"She tells him she's certain that he's the father. He

hangs up on her," says another writer.

Suddenly, all the writers are involved—everybody is throwing out scenes. The element of *conflict* has sparked real interest and a sense of excitement.

But not all the suggested scenes are accepted. We become demanding. We insist that the scenes (1) move the story forward, (2) are not familiar, (3) increase our *involvement* in the movie.

We are all in this together. We are *creating a movie we see in our heads.*

By chance, in this example, we have stumbled onto a universal theme (unwanted pregnancy) that can cause great stress and strong emotions. It is a deeply passionate and timeless theme with powerful political, and religious overtones. We can tell this story anytime in any place.

We see terrific possibilities in this premise; our creative juices are flowing. Suggested scenes come pouring out. At the same time, we become more selective—this is now *our* story.

One writer takes notes, keeps a scene-by-scene record of our progress. (Sometimes, when a story is hot, several writers write down the scenes.)

When the story being developed is very strong, it is continued through several sessions. When the game works, it is a joy to behold and exciting to participate in.

The Movie Game teaches the importance of cause and effect drama, as well as scene selection and omission. The writers quickly learn that a boring story is almost invariably due to a lack of conflict or dramatic tension.

The Movie Game is also an excellent aid for writers seeking a collaborator. Try playing the movie game with prospective writing partners. See if you spark each other; see if you share similar ideas about what makes a great movie and how you go about achieving your goal. The Movie Game will help you discover if you and your prospective partner have a good creative chemistry together. The test of every collaboration is whether the sum is greater than the parts. If not, you are better off working alone. Remember, in a collaboration, you will share not only all the income but all the credits. (In the Hollywood movie-making world, agents and buyers often conduct private discussions centered on a simple questions: "Which one of the collaborating duo *really* has the talent?")

What If Writing Exercises

All movie stories are created and developed from the writer's many "What if . . ." explorations.

Examples:

What if your protagonist takes a job that promises to bring him fame and fortune but also promises to destroy his marriage and his family?

What if your major character takes on a powerful political machine that has the power to blackmail him for past indiscretions?

What if an acclaimed drug-busting district attorney discovers his son is the neighborhood drug dealer?

What if two men and one woman on a fishing expedition are shipwrecked in a storm and survive by swimming ashore on a small tropical island? (What if one of the men is married to the woman and the other man has always coveted her?)

When working from a "What if . . ." premise you must first choose your genre. Any of the examples given above can be played as drama, melodrama, comedy, or even farce. If you have difficulty working on a story, you may discover that you have selected the wrong genre in which to tell it. Perhaps changing the genre will make your story work.

No matter what developmental methods you employ—
The Movie Game or "What if . . ." explorations—the most
important demand that you must make upon yourself
when developing your story is, at all costs, *avoid the ordinary, the predictable, the second rate. If you've seen it
before, don't write it.*

Conflict is the key element that you must find quickly
as you develop your story ideas.

A long-standing joke among screenwriting teachers is
that the first three rules of screenwriting are (1) structure,
(2) structure, (3) structure. I have come to believe that the
those are the *second* three rules. The first three rules of
screenwriting are (1) conflict, (2) conflict, (3) conflict.

David Webb Peoples' screenplay for *Unforgiven*, starring and directed by Clint Eastwood, is an excellent example of the power of conflict. Study this outstanding
film.

Remember, if you are not excited by the material you
are coming up with when working these exercises or
developing a story, move on to other story ideas. Above
all else, the storyteller must be completely captured by
his or her own story. Building a good story is hard work
but it also is fun. If you don't think that you can have fun
doing hard work, just ask any professional athlete.

If you feel certain that you know what the buyers and
the public will buy, the chances are that you are wrong. If
you commit yourself to work that you would pay to see,
you are probably on the right track.

As a screenwriter, you will spend your professional

life taking gambles on your own gut instincts. That's the way it must be. Nobody else can or should decide what you write. If you allow someone else to decide what you write, you will live to regret it.

Bet on yourself. Take the big gambles. Work freely and work hard. There is no other way to succeed in any field of endeavor, most especially in screenwriting.

Afterword

The annual Academy of Motion Picture Arts and Sciences Awards, the Oscars, have become essentially a popularity contest among the few thousand members of the Academy who work in Hollywood. However, sometimes Oscars are awarded solely on the basis of merit. In either case, Oscars generate an enormous amount of publicity and tremendous box-office returns worldwide. The ceremonies are viewed by an estimated *one billion people* on TV every year.

It is for this latter reason that I have included Oscar-winning or nominated screenplays wherever feasible as examples for this book. It is likely, because of the attention Oscar has given these movies, that most of my readers will have seen these movies in theatres rather than on videotape. Movies seen in theatres stick in the memory longer than those seen on the TV tube and generally have much more impact upon viewing.

I urge those of you who are interested in any kind of movie career to go to as many movies *in movie theatres* as your time and budget will allow. It is *still* the best way to learn the tricks of the trade.